The
South Carolina Colony

by Dennis Brindell Fradin

Consultant: Stephen Hoffius
South Carolina Historical Society
Charleston, South Carolina

CHILDRENS PRESS®
CHICAGO

Library of Congress Cataloging-in-Publication Data

Fradin, Dennis B.
   The South Carolina Colony / by Dennis B. Fradin.
      p.   cm. — (The thirteen colonies)
   Includes index.
   Summary: Describes the history and people of South Carolina from its
earliest settlements to statehood in 1788.
   ISBN 0-516-00397-6
   1. South Carolina—History—Colonial period, ca. 1600-1775—Juvenile
literature. 2. South Carolina—History—Revolution, 1775-1783—Juvenile
literature. [1. South Carolina—History—Colonial period, ca. 1600-1775.
2. South Carolina—History—Revolution, 1775-1783.] I. Title. II. Series: Fradin,
Dennis B. Thirteen colonies.
   F272.F72   1992
   975.7'03—dc20   91–32330
                                                                              CIP
                                                                              AC

April, 1992

Table of Contents

Magnolia Gardens, near Charleston, South Carolina. A white footbridge crosses Black Cypress Lake. Left: the state seal of South Carolina.

Chapter I

Introducing the Palmetto State

The Spring is a most delightful Season [in South Carolina]; our boundless Forests are then cloathed with Leaves, and enamelled with aromatic Flowers and Blossoms of the most lively Colors, perfuming the ambient Air; the winged Songsters chirping on every Bough, with enchanting Melody.

From A Short Description of the Province of South-Carolina, *written in 1763 by Dr. George Milligen Johnston*

South Carolina, a small state shaped like a leaf, is located in "the South," a region that makes up most of the southeastern United States. South Carolina is wedged between North Carolina, its "sister state," to the north, and Georgia to the south and west. To the east, more than 3,000 miles of Atlantic Ocean separate South Carolina from the coast of Africa.

It is fitting that South Carolina is leaf-shaped, because the state is famous for its beautiful plant life. When much of the northern United States is still blanketed by snow, flowers are blooming and trees are budding in South Carolina. Carolina jessamines (the state flower), azaleas, magnolias, camellias, and many other flowers help make South Carolina beautiful, as anyone who has been there in the springtime knows! Some of South Carolina's plant life helps give the state its Southern "look." For example, a kind of palm called the palmetto (the state tree) and the Spanish moss that hangs from many trees are typically Southern plants. And the Carolinas are the only two states where the Venus's-flytrap, a plant that "eats" insects, grows in the wild.

Each year, millions of tourists visit South Carolina. They swim, boat, and play golf at its coastal resorts, visit its lovely old plantations and historic sites, and enjoy its natural beauty. Few of these visitors realize that South Carolina has one of the most tragic histories of any state in the United States.

For thousands of years, Native Americans were the only people in South Carolina. In 1670, English people became the first permanent European colonists in South Carolina when they founded Charleston (which was called Charles Town in colonial times). With the founding of Charleston, South Carolina became the twelfth of England's thirteen American colonies to be

The palmetto tree is the emblem of South Carolina.

settled, following Virginia, Massachusetts, New Hampshire, New York, Connecticut, Maryland, Rhode Island, Delaware, Pennsylvania, North Carolina, and New Jersey, and ahead of only Georgia.

In all thirteen colonies, large numbers of people died of diseases that have since been conquered. Because its swamps bred so many germ-carrying insects, South Carolina had some terrible epidemics. At times, Charlestonians and other South Carolinians died by the hundreds from yellow fever and other diseases.

South Carolina's tragic history includes its treatment of Native Americans. Throughout colonial America, the settlers pushed the Native Americans off their lands, defeated them in bloody wars, and then enslaved some of them. South Carolinians probably enslaved more Native Americans than did the people of any other colony.

But South Carolina's largest-scale tragedy was the enslavement of African people. Although all thirteen colonies allowed slavery, no other colony relied as heavily as South Carolina upon this cruel practice. In the other colonies, the white people outnumbered the slaves. By 1750, two out of every three South Carolinians were slaves. The slaves grew the rice and the other crops that made

COLONIAL AMERICA

Map of the thirteen colonies

A Native American is hauled into slavery.

South Carolina prosperous, but their only reward was a life of hardship and misery.

One of South Carolina's proudest periods came during the Revolutionary War (1775–1783), which the Americans fought to free the thirteen colonies from England and turn them into the United States. Because of its success under English rule, South Carolina had less reason to be dissatisfied than nearly all of the other colonies. Yet many thousands of South Carolinians fought England, including such famous heroes as the "Swamp Fox" (Francis Marion) and the "Gamecock" (Thomas Sumter). The Palmetto State was also the scene of more than 100 Revolutionary War battles, including those fought at Camden, Kings Mountain, and Cowpens.

In 1787, soon after winning the Revolutionary War, the United States made a framework of government called the U.S. Constitution. By then the North had begun to end slavery, and many Northerners wanted the Constitution to outlaw slavery throughout the new United States. But because most white Southerners would have rejected such a constitution, slavery was allowed to continue in the nation.

By 1860, slavery had ended in the North, and white Southerners saw that the United States

Francis Marion, the Swamp Fox

Thomas Sumter, the Gamecock

government would soon end slavery throughout the country. Many Southerners opposed the U.S. government on other issues as well. So strongly did white Southerners feel about these matters that eleven Southern states seceded (withdrew) from the United States and formed their own country, the Confederate States of America. On December 20, 1860, South Carolina became the first state to leave the Union. This meant war, because the United States viewed the Confederates as rebels who had no right to secede.

On April 12, 1861, South Carolina was the scene of perhaps the saddest event in United States history. At 4:30 that morning, Confederate troops fired on Charleston's Fort Sumter, a U.S. military post. Those shots began the Civil War

South Carolina was the first state to leave the Union. The opening shots of the Civil War were fired at Charleston's Fort Sumter.

(1861–1865), in which Confederate (Southern) troops fought Union (Northern) soldiers. About 15,000 of South Carolina's 63,000 Confederate troops died in battle during the Civil War, the deadliest war in American history. Union troops also destroyed many South Carolina plantations and burned much of the state capital, Columbia, to the ground.

Following the Civil War, South Carolina had some very hard times. Poverty was widespread. And for many years, South Carolina had the nation's largest percentage of people who could not read or write, partly because the state made little effort to educate its black children. Even today, South Carolina has a very high rate of people who cannot read or write, and it still has a large proportion of poor people. However, the Palmetto State has experienced a rebirth in recent decades.

Much of this success is due to better education for everyone. Since the mid-1900s, South Carolina has been more concerned with educating all its children equally. Another boost has been South Carolina's transformation from a mainly farming to a mainly manufacturing state. South Carolina is still a leader in growing cotton, tobacco, and peaches, but it has also become a top-notch state for making textiles (cloth), clothing, and chemicals. Today, manufacturing provides many more jobs in South Carolina and brings in much more money than does farming. Manufacturing successes and better educational opportunities for everyone may enable this lovely state with the tragic past to enjoy a glorious future.

Tobacco and cotton (inset) are the two main agricultural crops in South Carolina today.

Chapter II

The Native Americans

The arrival of Europeans in this new World has been productive of the most ruinous consequences to [the Native Americans], who have lost their ancient Habitations, and the best of their Lands, either by the Force of Arms, or of trifling Presents made to them. . . . Many populous Tribes are already extinct, and their very Names forgot. The few that remain daily decrease in their Numbers, a Circumstance that gives them much concern, however agreeable it may be to the selfish and all-grasping Europeans.

From A Short Description of the Province of South-Carolina, *written in 1763 by Dr. George Milligen Johnston*

Native Americans first came to what is now South Carolina at least 10,000 years ago. Although the early people left behind no written records, items such as stone spearheads, pottery, log forts and homes, and large burial mounds provide us with clues about them. At first, the ancient people lived by hunting and fishing. By about 3,000 years ago, they had learned to farm. These ancient people may have been the ancestors of some of the state's modern Native American tribes.

Native American arrowheads and tools made of stone.

Before the arrival of Europeans, at least 20,000 Native Americans—and perhaps many more—belonging to as many as fifty tribes lived in South Carolina. The largest tribe was the Cherokee. *Cherokee* is thought to mean "Mountain People" or "Cave People," referring to the tribe's love of high regions. The Cherokee lived in mountainous parts of western South Carolina and in the high regions of North Carolina, Tennessee, Alabama, Georgia, and Virginia. Another major tribe, the Catawba, lived in central South Carolina and also in North Carolina. The Westo and Yamasee were two tribes that lived along the Savannah River which separates South Carolina from Georgia. The Kiawah and Wando lived around present-day Charleston, and the Congaree lived where the state capital, Columbia, now stands.

A map of South Carolina provides clues to the homelands of the Native Americans. Western South Carolina has a Cherokee County and a town named Cherokee Falls. The Catawba River (also known as the Wateree) runs down the center of South Carolina. Kiawah Island and the Wando River are near Charleston, while Columbia, the state capital, lies along the Congaree River.

The Native Americans lived in villages of a few dozen to several thousand people. They used wood

South Carolina

14

Native American villages were often surrounded by wooden walls called palisades.

and tree bark to build their dome-shaped or squarish homes. Along the coast, the people covered their walls and ceilings with marsh grass and palmetto leaves.

South Carolina had everything the Native Americans needed. The soil was fertile and the rivers teemed with trout, bass, and sturgeon. Woods and swamps in the region were filled with such animals as deer, bears, wild turkeys, and ducks, and with such plants as wild plums and cherries, blackberries, hickory nuts, and strawberries. In those bygone times, South Carolina was also home to several kinds of animals that we will never see, because people have wiped them

Native Americans caught fish with nets and spears.

out. One was a green, orange, and yellow bird called the Carolina parakeet; another was the passenger pigeon.

The Native Americans made great use of these natural resources. They grew corn, beans, and squash in the fertile soil. Usually the women did the farming, but in some tribes, including the Catawba, the men did much of the farm work. Children gathered berries and nuts in the forest, and scared birds away from the growing crops. Men fished in the rivers with poles and nets, and hunted in the woods and wetlands with bows and arrows and traps.

Animals and plants provided the Native Americans with much more than food. Animal skins were made into clothes, blankets, and moccasins. Moss was perfect for making babies' diapers. Small bones were transformed into needles, turtle shells became bowls, and bird feathers made beautiful decorations. The Native Americans also used plants to make medicines. For example, they made a kind of aspirin out of willow bark.

The Native Americans differed from the Europeans in several major ways. For one thing, they believed in many spirits instead of one God. As best we can tell, many of the Native Americans believed in two main gods—the Great Spirit and the Evil Spirit. The Great Spirit was thought to provide the good things in life, including fine weather and large harvests. The Evil Spirit was blamed for bad weather and poor harvests. The tribes also believed that every star, animal, stream, and mountain had a spirit.

The Native Americans held a number of yearly festivals to honor their spirits. The Green Corn Dance was held each summer to thank the spirits for the first corn of the season. The New Year's

In winter, the Native Americans wore robes of deerskin.

John White's drawing shows a ceremonial dance of the Carolina people

Dance, which came in late November, was an important Cherokee festival. At New Year's, the sacred fire in each Cherokee town was put out and a new fire was lit for the upcoming year. With the lighting of the new fire, people were supposed to forget old grudges and make a fresh start with everyone. The Native Americans danced, sang, prayed, and feasted at their religious festivals. They smoked a plant the Cherokee called *tsalu* (meaning "fire in the mouth") in the belief that the smoke carried their prayers up to the spirits.

However, the Indians did not smoke *tsalu* (tobacco) as a daily habit.

The Native Americans also had a much different way of raising children. Most Europeans of the 1600s believed in harsh discipline for young people. Native American parents, on the other hand, rarely hit or even yelled at their children. They were afraid that the spirits might think the children were unwanted and snatch them back to the spirit world. The Native Americans had no schools for their children, either. Boys learned to hunt, fish, and make canoes and weapons by working alongside their uncles. Girls learned to cook, make clothes, and grow crops by helping their mothers.

Children learned tribal beliefs from stories told by the elders. The Cherokee had an interesting creation story. According to the legend, the animals lived in the sky above the water-covered Earth long before there were people. When the animals' Sky World became crowded, Water Beetle dived down into the Water World and brought up some mud. The mud became the world's land. The Great Buzzard then flew down to explore, but after a while he grew tired and flew too low. In places, his wings beat up ridges. The ridges became the world's mountains. The first people—

a young man and woman—were made sometime later. There were only these two people until the man poked the woman in the side with a fish, causing her to have a baby seven days later. For a while she had a new baby every seven days. Then, seeing that the world would be too crowded if this continued, the spirits arranged that a woman could give birth only once every nine months.

The Native Americans and the Europeans also had widely contrasting views about land and war. To the Native Americans, land was like the air— something that everyone shared and no one owned. In fact, across colonial America the Native Americans were at first happy to share the land with the early settlers. They had no inkling that the people they treated so generously would someday want *all* the land for themselves.

As for war, few people understand the Native Americans' views on this subject even now. Generally, Native Americans went out of their way to help friends, relatives, and even strangers. Now and then, though, a tribe or village felt so seriously wronged that it went to war against an enemy. When that happened, the Native Americans were ruthless. They attacked their enemies whenever they could, even when they were sleeping.

Native Americans shooting burning moss into an enemy village to set the thatched roofs on fire

The Europeans who arrived in the 1600s believed in a code of warfare in which two armies met on a field and fought.

Young Indian men trained for war by playing rugged sports and games. One popular sport among the South Carolina tribes was a forerunner of lacrosse. Wooden goalposts were set up

Young men trained for battle by running, playing games, and practicing with the bow and arrow.

on both sides of a field. Using sticks with a leather web attached to the end, two teams tried to send the deerskin ball through each other's goal. The players couldn't use their hands, but they were allowed to strike one another with their sticks. This game was so brutal that it was known as "Little Brother to War." Tribes sometimes settled disputes by playing a game of "Little Brother to War," with the winners getting their way in the argument. The Cherokee loved a game they called *gatayusti*, which was played by rolling disk-shaped stones on the ground and then trying to hit them with spears.

The Native Americans had leaders known as *chiefs*. Most of them were men, but at one time the Congaree had a woman chief. The chiefs were less powerful than they are usually portrayed in movies and stories. Generally, they advised and helped guide their people, but major decisions were made by the whole village. One tactic the Europeans used was to pick out a man who claimed to be chief and give him gifts in return for land. Often the person wasn't really a chief, but the colonists would then push the Native Americans off the land because the "chief" had made a deal with them.

The colonists were cruel to the Native Americans throughout America, but nowhere was their treatment of them more savage than in South Carolina. There, colonists enslaved and murdered Native Americans by the thousands, and then cheated the survivors out of vast tracts of land. Today only about 10,000 Native Americans live in the Palmetto State, some of them unrelated to the people who lived there long ago.

An expedition led by Jean Ribault enters the St. John River to claim Florida for France. The discoveries of Christopher Columbus (left) opened the New World to European explorers and settlers.

Chapter III

Explorers and First Settlers

The Heavens shine upon this famous Country the sovereign Ray of health; and has blest it with a serene Air, and a lofty Sky....

From A True Description of Carolina, *by Joel Gascoyne (1674)*

Who was the first European explorer to reach what is now the United States? That is one of the mysteries of history. The Vikings of Norway and nearby lands may have reached what is now the United States around A.D. 1000. If they did, it was probably the northeastern part of the region rather than the Carolinas.

The Vikings did not build any lasting settlements, and whatever knowledge they had of the New World was lost to nearly all Europeans for hundreds of years. About 500 years passed before the next European reached the New World. His name was Christopher Columbus, and he was an Italian explorer working for Spain. But Columbus never reached what is now the United States, either on his voyage of 1492 or on any of his three

Amerigo Vespucci

later voyages. Instead, Columbus explored parts of Central and South America and also islands off the coast of Florida.

In fact, Columbus never knew the true nature of the Americas. All his life he thought he had reached the continent of Asia—specifically, the *Indies*, as the region of India, China, and Japan was known back then. Convinced that he had landed in the Indies, Columbus called the people of the region *Indians*. Even though it was based on wrong information, the name stuck, and to this day the islands between Florida and South America are called the *West Indies* because Columbus thought they were located somewhere near India!

The Italian sailor Amerigo Vespucci was the first European to realize the true nature of the New World. While Amerigo was on a voyage to South America for Portugal in 1501–02, it dawned on him that the land stretched too far south to be Asia. Because Amerigo Vespucci figured out what they were, North and South America were given his first name, with a slight change in spelling.

Columbus's voyages paved the way for Spain to colonize much of Central and South America as well as the West Indies. The Spanish grew rich from their American colonies. They sent treasure

Native American prisoners make a break for freedom by jumping from a Spanish ship.

ships heaped with gold and silver back to Spain, and built many large farms known as plantations in the New World. All this was done at the expense of the Native Americans, whom the Spaniards enslaved and killed by the tens of thousands.

Spain was not as interested in the present-day United States as it was in lands to the south. However, the Spanish did explore and colonize some parts of what are now the southern and southwestern United States in the early 1500s.

The first known Europeans in South Carolina were Spaniards from what is now the island country of the Dominican Republic in the West Indies. Led by Francisco Gordillo, the Spaniards reached the South Carolina coast in 1521. The Spaniards named the region *Carolana* (meaning "land of Charles" in Latin) for Spain's King Charles I. By chance, the English king Charles I later gave the same name to the Carolinas.

Exploration wasn't the Spaniards' only goal. They had killed so many of their slaves in the West Indies that they wanted to capture more Native Americans. At the mouth of the Pee Dee River, where Georgetown, South Carolina, now stands, the visitors played a cruel trick. First the Spaniards captured two Native Americans and took them aboard a Spanish ship. The Spanish showered the captives with gifts and treated them royally. Then they invited about 150 other Native Americans onto their ships, promising them similar gifts. Once these people were aboard, the Spaniards set sail for the West Indies.

One of the kidnapped Indians learned Spanish and made friends with Francisco Gordillo, who liked him so much that he named him Francisco

Chicora, after himself. Francisco Chicora became a personal servant to Lucas Vásquez de Ayllón, an important Spanish official in the West Indies. Francisco Chicora told Ayllón some strange tales that the Spaniard apparently believed. In the Carolana region, Francisco Chicora claimed, there lived a people who had tails. When they sat down, they rested their tails in holes in the ground! Francisco Chicora also explained that another tribe in the area made their children into giants by stretching them! Perhaps what interested Ayllón most were Francisco Chicora's stories about all the treasure that abounded in Carolana. Ayllón took Francisco Chicora with him to Spain, where King Charles I gave the Spaniard permission to found a large colony in Carolana.

King Charles I of Spain, also known as Emperor Charles V of the Holy Roman Empire

In 1526 Ayllón led an expedition consisting of more than 500 people and many farm animals from what is now the Dominican Republic to Carolana. At first the colonists settled at an unknown spot along the coast of what are now the Carolinas. Because of starvation and disease, Ayllón moved the colony to a spot somewhere along the South Carolina coast, probably on Winyah Bay near present-day Georgetown. That didn't help. By the fall of 1526 Ayllón and more than two-thirds of his colonists were dead. In

Giovanni da Verrazano

October 1526, the surviving 150 colonists returned to the West Indies.

Meanwhile, France had also become interested in colonizing America. In 1524 Giovanni da Verrazano, an Italian working for France, explored the east coast of what is now the United States. France then made several attempts to build settlements along the coast. Jean Ribault, a Frenchman, worked out a plan to settle French Huguenots (Protestants who were persecuted by France's Catholic-controlled government) in what is now the southeastern United States. In February 1562, Ribault led 150 men who were mostly

Jean Ribault and his French Huguenot settlers land in South Carolina.

Huguenots like himself on a voyage from France to America.

Ribault and his men landed in Florida and then sailed northward. In late spring they reached Parris Island along Port Royal Sound in southeastern South Carolina. There they built a military post called Charlesfort. Ribault left twenty-six men at Charlesfort, then returned to France with the others to obtain more settlers and supplies.

Those twenty-six Frenchmen turned out to be poor colonists. They failed to plant crops and might have starved if not for friendly Native Americans. Also, the soldier left in charge of the little colony was a tyrant. He hanged one man for making a remark he disliked, and abandoned another man, known as La Chere, on a deserted island a few miles from the fort. The colonists were so angry at their cruel leader that they killed him and rescued La Chere.

Week after week passed with no sign of Ribault, who had been prevented from returning by troubles in France. Finally, in the spring of 1563 the Frenchmen abandoned their colony. They cut down trees and built a boat, using their shirts and sheets for sails. The men tried to sail back to France, but partway across the ocean they ran out

The Huguenot settlers built a boat and tried to sail back to France.

of food. In desperation, they ate their shoes and leather jackets. After several men had died of hunger, they realized that someone must give his life for the sake of the others. They drew lots, and La Chere lost. He was killed and eaten. It was said that by the time the survivors were picked up by an English ship, they had lost their minds.

The Spanish colony that Ayllón had begun in South Carolina in 1526 and the French colony that Ribault had founded in 1562 were two historical "almosts." Had either colony survived, it would have been the first permanent European settlement in what is now the United States. Instead, that honor went to St. Augustine, Florida, which the Spanish founded in 1565.

The New World according to a mapmaker of 1540

Spain still hoped to colonize the South Carolina region. In 1566—the year after the founding of St. Augustine—the Spaniards built Fort San Felipe on Parris Island not far from the abandoned French Charlesfort. Fort San Felipe did not last long, partly because of conflicts the Spaniards set off with the Native Americans. It also appears that in the late 1570s the French built a fort near present-day Charleston that was abandoned rather quickly.

English people proved to be the Carolinas' first permanent colonists, but only after a long struggle. England's claim to America was based on a voyage made by John Cabot in 1497. Nearly a century passed before England acted on its claim. Then in 1585 Walter Raleigh sent out about 600 men to plant England's first colony in America. The fort and cottages they built on North Carolina's Roanoke Island might have become England's first permanent American colony were it not for the newcomers' cruelty and stupidity. One of the Englishmen's drinking cups was missing, and they suspected that a Native American had stolen it. In revenge, the Englishmen burned the tribe's village and cornfields. After seeing what the Englishmen would do over a missing drinking cup, not even Native Americans who had been friendly toward them would give the colonists the food they needed. The Englishmen had to abandon this colony in 1586.

The next year, 1587, Walter Raleigh sent another expedition to Roanoke Island. They had been there only a few days when Eleanor White Dare gave birth to a baby girl—the first English child born in North America. The baby had been born in what is now North Carolina, but the English called the lands that became Virginia, the Carolinas, and several other states *Virginia*. For that reason, the baby's parents named her Virginia Dare.

Unfortunately, Virginia Dare and the rest of the colonists on Roanoke Island mysteriously disappeared. Because we don't know what happened to them, they are known as the Lost Colony.

The English didn't give up their plans to colonize America, however. In 1607 they finally founded their first permanent American colony at Jamestown, Virginia. Over the next few years, English people settled other colonies along the east coast. The groundwork for permanent English colonization of the Carolinas was laid in 1629, when King Charles I of England gave a huge chunk of America to Sir Robert Heath, an important official in England. In those days England's

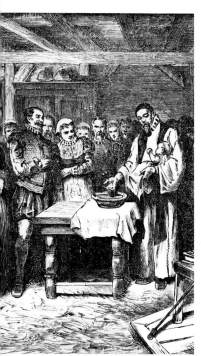

The baptism of Virginia Dare

rulers assumed the right to not only grant but also name American land. King Charles I named Heath's territory *Carolana*, after himself, which meant that the region kept the name it had been given by the Spaniards.

Carolana in 1629 was much larger than present-day North and South Carolina. Not only was Georgia part of Carolana, but the territory stretched all the way west to the Pacific Ocean. As it turned out, the Carolinas gave up their claim to Georgia and the western lands. If they hadn't, the cities of Atlanta (Georgia), Birmingham (Alabama), Little Rock (Arkansas), Lubbock (Texas), Phoenix (Arizona), and Los Angeles (California) would all be part of South Carolina today!

Sir Robert Heath planned to colonize Carolana with French Huguenots—the people Jean Ribault had tried to settle in the region about seventy years earlier. But Heath couldn't obtain the money needed to build a settlement, and so Carolana remained uncolonized for another generation. Not until the early 1650s did some English people from Virginia trickle down into the region. By 1660 about 1,000 Europeans lived in Carolana—

King Charles I of England

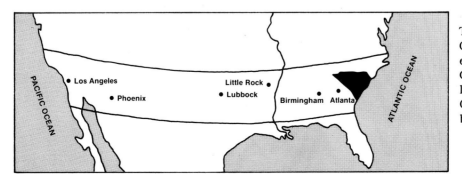

The huge territory of Carolina originally extended to the Pacific Ocean. The part that later became South Carolina is shown in black.

King Charles II of England

all of them in what in now North Carolina. Present-day South Carolina wasn't permanently settled for another ten years.

Events that took place thousands of miles away in England led to the settlement of South Carolina. Charles I, the king who had given Carolana to Heath, was beheaded in 1649. For more than a decade thereafter, England was ruled by powerful lawmakers instead of by a king or queen. All that time, people who were loyal to the dead Charles I tried to crown his son, Charles II, as king of England. Charles II finally took the throne in 1660. He rewarded some of the people who had been loyal to his family by giving them land in America.

In 1663, King Charles II changed the spelling of *Carolana* by one letter to *Carolina*. That same year, he also granted Carolina to eight of his most loyal noblemen. Their names were Edward Hyde, Earl of Clarendon; George Monck, Duke of Albemarle; Anthony Ashley Cooper; William, Earl of Craven; Sir George Carteret; Sir John Colleton; and two brothers, Sir William Berkeley and John, Lord Berkeley. The eight men became Carolina's Lords Proprietors, or landlords, and Carolina was now a proprietary (privately owned) colony. A number of place-names in the Carolinas remind us of these long-ago landlords. For example, South Carolina has Berkeley, Clarendon, and Colleton counties, as well as the Ashley and Cooper rivers.

Seal of the Lords Proprietors of Carolina

The Lords Proprietors had a motive for wanting to settle Carolina—money! Settlers who rented land in Carolina had to pay the Proprietors a small fee called a quitrent. Those who purchased their land had to buy it from the Proprietors. The Proprietors tried to make Carolina as attractive as possible. In 1669 they put the Fundamental Constitutions into effect. Among other things, this frame of government opened Carolina to people of all religions. Although Americans take freedom of religion for granted today, this idea was ahead of its time in 1669. Many of the other colonies banned or persecuted Quakers, Jews, and other people who didn't belong to the Church of England (the official religion in England). From the start, Carolina welcomed such people. Many historians feel that only Rhode Island offered more religious freedom than Carolina.

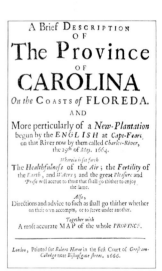

The title page of *A Brief Description of the Province of Carolina*, which told of the wonders of the new colony.

Cheap land and the opportunity to worship freely attracted thousands of people to the Carolinas in the late 1600s. In 1669 the Lords Proprietors signed up more than 100 people to become South Carolina's first permanent settlers. That summer these people packed their belongings and sailed from England aboard three ships—the *Carolina*, the *Port Royal*, and the *Albemarle*. The expedition, which stopped in the West Indies before heading north to Carolina, was slammed by storms that wrecked the *Albemarle* and the *Port Royal*. Apparently none of the colonists died in these storms, but the expedition was delayed. Not until March 1670 did the *Carolina* and a ship that had been rented in Bermuda reach the South Carolina coast. It had taken the settlers half a year to reach their destination.

The Proprietors wanted the colonists to build their first town along Port Royal Sound in what is now southeastern South Carolina. This was the area where the French had built Charlesfort and the Spaniards had built Fort San Felipe. But the leaders of the expedition opposed this idea. The Spanish had outposts in both Florida and Georgia by this time. Wanting to put a little more distance between themselves and the Spaniards, the newcomers sailed about fifty miles farther up the South Carolina coast. There, along a river the Native Americans called the Kiawah and the English called the Ashley, the settlers marked off streets and cut down trees to build fortifications and homes. This first town in South Carolina was briefly known as Albemarle Point, but after about a year its name was changed to Charles Town, after England's King Charles II. This old name is sometimes also written Charles-town, Charles-Town, or Charlestown, but for simplicity we are using the spelling that became official in 1783—Charleston.

Over the next few years, more English people moved to Charleston. They came from England and also from Barbados, an English-ruled island in the West Indies. The early colonists planted corn, potatoes, and other food crops, but it seems that many of them were new at farming because they suffered from food shortages. Fortunately, a colonist named Dr. Henry Woodward had lived with the Native Americans in South Carolina for a time before the founding of Charleston, and was well liked by them. Woodward traded with the Native Americans for corn and other provisions that the settlers at Charleston needed.

Another problem was that many of the colonists found it difficult to do their own farm work. They were unable to cope with the heat, and they succumbed in large numbers to the outbreaks of malaria and yellow fever caused by mosquitoes that bred in the swamps. However, the settlers found a way to farm without doing the work themselves. Two groups of people—the Native Americans and the Africans—were accustomed to living in a region with South Carolina's climate and hazards. Slavery was legal in South Carolina from the start. Within a few years, hundreds of black slaves had been brought to South Carolina either directly from Africa or from Africa by way of Barbados. South Carolina eventually had a larger percentage of black slaves among its people than any other American colony. What is less widely known is that South Carolinians were also the leading slave traders of Native Americans in what is now the United States. The Lords Proprietors called South Carolinians who captured and sold Indians "evil men," but that didn't stop them.

By 1680 South Carolina was home to about 1,000 white colonists, about 200 black slaves, and an unknown number of Native American slaves. Charleston, which was still the colony's only town, had a change in location that year. The original site had been unhealthy because of swamps. In 1680 the settlers moved Charleston a short way east to a tract of land between the Ashley and the Cooper rivers. Soon Charleston would be one of colonial America's leading towns, and South Carolina would be one of the most successful of the thirteen colonies.

DR. HENRY WOODWARD (about 1646–about 1686)

The little that we know about Henry Woodward tells us that his life would make a great adventure movie. Woodward may have been born on Barbados. At a very young age he became a surgeon, a profession that required little training in those days. Around the age of twenty, he moved to the North Carolina region, which had been permanently colonized for only a few years. Woodward soon volunteered for an expedition to present-day South Carolina to explore the area and establish friendly relations with the Native Americans.

Woodward and some other men set out from North Carolina in June 1666. While on this expedition, Henry Woodward was invited by Native Americans along the South Carolina coast to live with them for a time. Woodward accepted, thus becoming the first English person to call South Carolina home. He was one of the very few Englishmen who truly liked and respected Native Americans.

The Spaniards in Florida were disturbed to learn that Dr. Woodward was living peacefully with the South Carolina Indians. They were afraid that he would help the English gain a toehold in the area, which they hoped to rule themselves. The Spaniards sent out an expedition that captured Woodward. The doctor was taken to St. Augustine, Florida, where he was imprisoned. But a few months later, an English sea captain raided St. Augustine, releasing Dr. Woodward and others held prisoner by the Spaniards. Woodward was taken to the West Indies, where he worked as a ship's surgeon for a while. He hoped to save enough money to pay for a trip to England, but in the summer of 1669 his vessel was struck by a hurricane and he was shipwrecked at the island of Nevis in the West Indies.

But something always seemed to turn up for Henry Woodward! The expedition that left England in 1669 to build the first settlement in South Carolina stopped in the West Indies. Woodward joined the expedition and sailed to South Carolina. Since he had lived there and knew the Native Americans, he was very helpful to the English founders of Charleston. He obtained food for the colony from the Native Americans, and also made treaties with them.

Over the next few years, Dr. Woodward explored South Carolina and other parts of the South. He helped set up trade between the English and the Native Americans, and was partly responsible for the generally good relations between the two groups in early colonial times. Woodward also went out searching for gold and silver and had many other interesting adventures during his short life. It is thought that he died in the Charleston area at about the age of forty. Dr. Henry Woodward was married twice and his many famous descendants include at least three South Carolina governors.

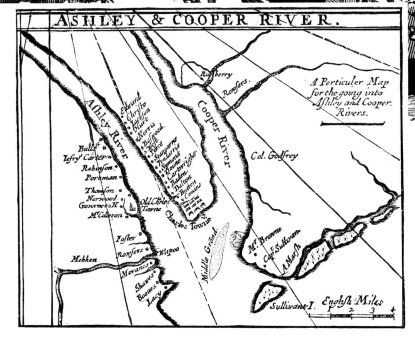

Old Charles Town was abandoned, and the settlers moved the town to a point of land between the Ashley and Cooper rivers (see map). The map shows the names of the landowners along the riverbanks.

Chapter IV

South Carolina's Youth: 1680–1729

For Gentility, politeness, and a handsome way of Living the Colony exceeds what I have seen.

Reverend Francis LeJau, writing about South Carolina in 1706

At first nearly all of the South Carolina colonists were of English heritage. Starting in the 1680s, large numbers of non-English people migrated to the colony. Many of them were from Scotland, the nation just north of England. In 1682, the Scotsman Henry Erskine, who was also called Lord Cardross, obtained a tract in South Carolina. In 1683 Lord Cardross led about 150 Scots to South Carolina to found what he hoped would be a large Scottish community. These people built Stuart Town just south of where Beaufort, South Carolina, now stands, but the town was not successful and it was destroyed in a Spanish invasion in 1686. Scottish people kept moving to South Carolina, though, so in a way Lord Cardross's dream came true. By the end of colonial times about one in every seven white South Carolinians was of Scottish background. Only Georgia and North Carolina had a comparable proportion of Scottish people.

French Huguenots—the people Jean Ribault and Sir Robert Heath had wanted to send to South Carolina—finally began moving to the colony in large numbers in the 1680s. Along the banks of the Santee River north of Charleston, the Huguenots built a settlement called James Town. Although James Town, like Stuart Town, did not last, there were perhaps 500 French Huguenots in South Carolina by the year 1700.

Nearly all of the early colonists farmed. They grew a great deal of corn and also raised cattle. In fact, although we usually think of cowboys as originating in the American West, the African slaves who tended the cattle in South Carolina were among America's first cowboys. For its first few years, South Carolina lacked a big money-making farm product, such as tobacco was to Virginia and Maryland. This changed with the development of rice farming in the late 1600s, but there is disagreement about how this came about.

According to one story, a sea captain brought some rice seeds from Africa to Charleston during the 1680s. He gave the seeds to a Mr. Woodward

Slaves unloading rice barges. Some riverside plantations shipped their goods directly to England from their own piers.

(thought by many to be Dr. Henry Woodward), who in turn divided them among people he knew. According to a second story, a ship carrying rice was wrecked on the South Carolina coast. Farmers gathered the rice and planted it. There is also evidence in the form of a letter written in 1726 that "it was by a woman that Rice was transplanted into Carolina." Regardless of how it got there, rice grew beautifully in South Carolina's swampy land. By 1700 many farmers near the South Carolina coast were growing rice, which was becoming the colony's most important crop.

South Carolina produced some of the tastiest rice in the world. The rice that wasn't eaten by South Carolinians was sold to other American colonies, England, and the West Indies. There was a shortage of coins and printed money in colonial times. For a while in the 1700s rice was used instead of money to pay debts and taxes in South Carolina, as tobacco was used in Maryland and Virginia.

South Carolina's rice planters built huge plantations and imported large numbers of slaves to grow their rice crops. For example, Sir Nathaniel Johnson, governor of South Carolina from 1703 to 1709, brought more than 100 slaves into the colony during the 1690s. By about 1708, South Carolina's black slaves outnumbered its white people. This situation, which lasted for the rest of the colonial era, made white South Carolinians very nervous.

South Carolina's government consisted of a governor and a two-house legislature made up of the Council and the Commons House of Assembly. In 1696 the colonial government passed a slave code for South Carolina. One law ordered that slaves must have a written pass to leave home. Another ordered masters to regularly search slave huts for weapons. The code also spelled out

Slaves plowing a rice paddy

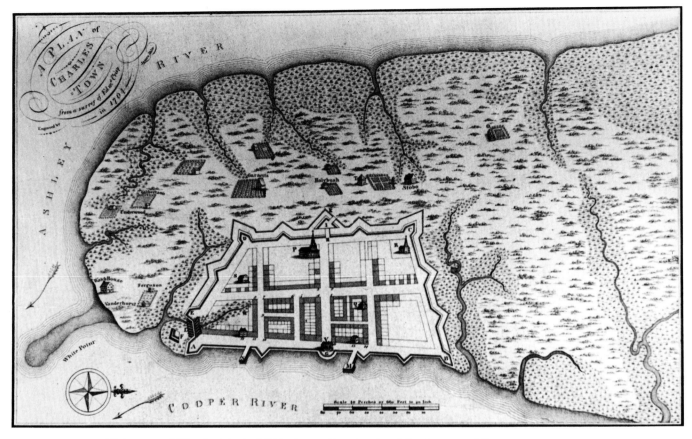

This map of Charleston in 1704 shows the streets of the town and the outlying farms.

punishments, including whipping and nose-slitting, for slaves who ran away.

The rice planters who lived in the Charleston area helped build the South Carolina capital into one of the leading towns in the thirteen colonies. By 1710, Charleston was home to several thousand people, and its fine port was constantly busy with shipping activities. Ships brought molasses, wine, fine clothes, and slaves into the colony. Then they carried rice, beef, deerskins, and naval stores (tar and other tree products used in building and repairing ships) out of South Carolina.

In 1710, a second permanent town, Beaufort, was laid out near the ocean in southeastern South Carolina. It was named for the Duke of Beaufort, one of the Lords Proprietors at that time.

Despite its success, South Carolina was the scene of tremendous turmoil. The colonists fought over religion and politics. The branches of government were often at each other's throats. And the Proprietors had trouble getting the colonists to follow their orders.

Some planters from Barbados lived near Charleston. They were called the Goose Creek Men because they made their homes along a branch of the Cooper River called Goose Creek. The Goose Creek Men, who controlled many political offices, did not believe in freedom of worship. They were Church of Englanders and felt that the Proprietors had been foolish to offer religious freedom to everyone in the colony. The Proprietors and some of the colonists clashed bitterly with the Goose Creek Men over their religious bigotry, their involvement in the Native American slave trade, and their trade with pirates.

When it came to governors, South Carolina may have set a record with how quickly they came and went, sometimes against their will! Many of the colonists did not want to pay the quitrents, and felt that the Proprietors should do more to defend South Carolina from the Spaniards and the Native Americans. As the Proprietors' representative in South Carolina, the governor received the brunt of the people's anger. However, it must also be said that some of the governors were selfish rascals.

Governor James Colleton was not only thrown out of office in 1690 but banished from the colony. The next governor, Seth Sothel, was worse. For much of the 1680s Sothel had governed North Carolina, where he made himself hated for taking bribes, seizing other people's land, and jailing his opponents. In 1689 North Carolina had placed him on trial for his actions, found him guilty, and thrown him out of the colony. So what did Sothel do? He went to South Carolina, where the Goose Creek Men helped him become governor. Sothel was soon up to his old tricks. The Proprietors disliked him so much that in 1691 they kicked him out of office and voided all the laws made

Seth Sothel and his followers took over the South Carolina government

during his term. Thus, Sothel had been booted out of the governorship of both Carolinas within two years! The next time someone says that today's lawmakers aren't as good as those from the "good old days," tell him or her about Seth Sothel!

Meanwhile, the three parts of government—governor, Council, and Commons House of Assembly—were squabbling. The government was designed so that the governor and the Council that helped him would have the bulk of the power in making and enforcing laws. At first the Commons House of Assembly, which tended to represent the less-wealthy people, had little power, and was not even allowed to propose laws. The Commons House fought and scratched for more power. In the 1690s it won the right to propose laws, and by late colonial times it had made itself more powerful than not only the Council but also the governor.

The people and governments of the Carolinas faced two big threats during the early 1700s—one on land and the other at sea. By the early 1700s the Native Americans had endured many torments at the hands of the Carolinians. They had been captured and sold as slaves, shortchanged when selling deerskins to white traders, and cheated in deals for their homelands. In 1711 North Carolina's Tuscarora nation decided to fight back. That September they attacked and killed about 140 North Carolinians, beginning what was called the Tuscarora War (1711–13).

One method the colonists used in fighting the Native Americans was to befriend a tribe that was an enemy of the tribe they were fighting. Then the colonists had the enemy tribe do much of their dirty work. North Carolinians used more than 1,000 Yamasee and other Native Americans from

South Carolina, along with a small number of South Carolina colonists, to help them fight the Tuscarora. By the spring of 1713 this combined fighting force had killed and captured hundreds of Tuscarora. But the Yamasee themselves were so badly treated by the South Carolina traders that they, too, soon planned to make war on the colonists.

In the spring of 1715, a Yamasee named Sanute warned a Mrs. Fraser of the Beaufort region that his people were about to attack. Sanute told Mrs. Fraser to flee to Charleston. Mrs. Fraser, along with her husband and child, did go to Charleston, but unfortunately they didn't tell other people about Sanute's warning. A few days later, on April 15, 1715, the Yamasee suddenly attacked and killed about 100 settlers in the Beaufort area, starting the Yamasee War (1715–17). Many other tribes helped the Yamasee fight the colonists. For a while, South Carolina appeared to be in danger of total destruction. About 400 South Carolina settlers were killed in the war, but in the end the colonists won, killing several hundred Native Americans. South Carolina was never weaker than it was after peace was made with the Native Americans in late 1717. Because many people had sought refuge in Charleston, farm fields had been

Sanute warned Mrs. Fraser about the Yamasee attack.

neglected during the war, resulting in widespread hunger. One colonist wrote that the colonists in Charleston were "ready to eat up one another for want of provisions."

The threat at sea came from pirates. Although they are often portrayed as romantic figures in films and books, pirates were actually robbers who worked at sea. Ship owners suffered from piracy, as did the merchants and planters whose goods were stolen. But many people gained from piracy, and some colonies welcomed these sea robbers. Pirates sold goods cheaply, spent their money freely when they came to town, and were willing to pay lawmakers large bribes to ignore their activities.

North Carolina's governor Charles Eden befriended the notorious pirate called Blackbeard, who reportedly shared his loot with the governor. In South Carolina, Governor Seth Sothel traded with the pirates, and a number of other lawmakers were soft on piracy. By and large, though, North Carolina was more tolerant of pirates than South Carolina because North Carolina didn't do much shipping. Few of the merchants, rich planters, and ship owners who suffered most from piracy lived in North Carolina. But South Carolina had many such citizens by 1700—the year seven pirates were hanged in the colony. Over the next few years many more pirates would be executed in South Carolina.

The most feared pirate in Carolina waters was Edward Teach, known as Blackbeard because of the long black beard that he braided and tied with colored ribbons. To make himself look as frightful as possible, Blackbeard placed slow-burning matches under his hat to make it look like his head was smoking! And Blackbeard's actions were as devilish as his looks. Victims who didn't hand over their rings when he robbed their ships reportedly lost both the rings *and* the fingers they were on. It was also said that Blackbeard shot at his own men now and then to remind them that he was the boss. Blackbeard robbed many ships along the coasts of the Carolinas, Virginia, and Delaware from about 1717 to 1718.

Blackbeard

Another man who terrorized ships along the same coastline at that time was Stede Bonnet, known as the Gentleman Pirate because he had been an officer in the British army and a rich planter on Barbados. People claimed that Bonnet became a pirate to escape his wife's nagging. Whether or not that was true, Bonnet could match Blackbeard for cruelty. He was one of only a few pirates who actually made his victims "walk the plank" (leap to their death in the ocean).

Something Blackbeard did in mid-1718 convinced many people that piracy must end. Around June 1, he sailed four ships manned by more than 400 pirates into South Carolina waters off Charleston. Within about a week, he robbed eight or nine vessels entering and leaving Charleston, and took the passengers and crew of one ship captive. Blackbeard needed medicine for sick members of his crew. He sent a message to South Carolina governor Robert Johnson that unless he was provided with a chest of medicines, he would send the governor the heads of his captives—among whom were some prominent Charlestonians, including lawmaker Samuel Wragg and his four-year-old son, William. Blackbeard also threatened to pound Charleston with his ships' guns and burn the vessels he had captured. The governor and his Council sent the medicines out to Blackbeard in the nick of time. Blackbeard's captives were stripped of their clothes and valuables, but at least they still had their heads.

After this, many Virginians and South Carolinians and a lesser number of North Carolinians were determined to stamp out piracy. In September 1718 South Carolina's governor Robert Johnson sent Colonel William Rhett to

Robert Maynard returns in triumph after defeating and killing Blackbeard.

hunt down the pirates. Rhett fought a sea battle with Stede Bonnet along the North Carolina coast. The "Gentleman Pirate" was captured and taken to Charleston. In a weird turn of events, Bonnet escaped wearing women's clothes, but was quickly recaptured.

Shortly after Bonnet was captured, Virginia governor Alexander Spotswood sent Lieutenant Robert Maynard of the British navy to fight Blackbeard. On November 22, 1718, the ships of Maynard and Blackbeard fought a ferocious sea battle along the North Carolina coast. Blackbeard and about ten of his men were killed, and the remaining fourteen were taken to Virginia, where they were tried and then hanged. Stede Bonnet and about fifty other captured pirates were hanged in Charleston in November and December 1718. Several pirates who were badly wounded were tried and hanged quickly—the South Carolinians didn't want them to die of their wounds before they could be executed!

There was a big governmental change in the Carolinas in the early 1700s. Although people had referred to "North Carolina" and "South Carolina" as separate since about 1690, technically there was still just one Carolina colony. South Carolina, which was one of America's richest regions, dominated North Carolina, which was one of the poorest. Even the Lords Proprietors favored the South Carolina region. For example, between 1691 and 1712 the Proprietors allowed the governor in Charleston to appoint a deputy to govern North Carolina. Finally, in 1712, the colony was formally divided into North Carolina and South Carolina.

This medal was struck to commemorate the 1712 separation of North and South Carolina.

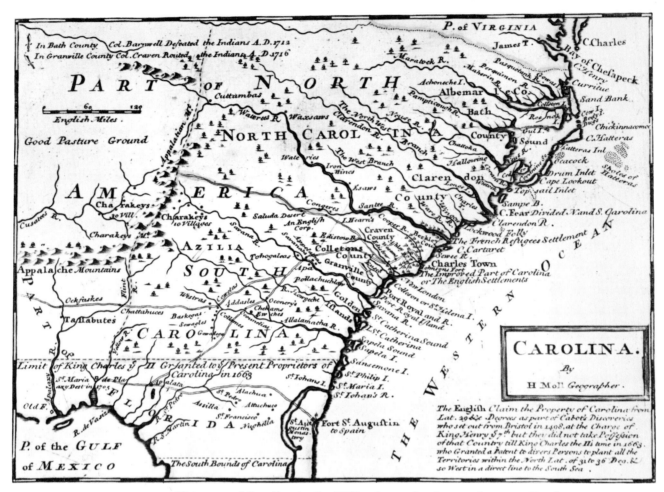

This map of Carolina in the 1720s shows the division between North and South Carolina.

The Proprietors then began appointing the North Carolina governor themselves.

Although they clashed on many other issues, North and South Carolinians agreed on their dislike of the Proprietors. They were angry that the Proprietors had raised the quitrents a number of times, and they felt that the Proprietors didn't do enough to protect them. In 1719 word reached

Charleston that the Spaniards were planning to attack the town. Realizing that the Proprietors wouldn't send help, the South Carolinians rebelled. Many of them signed a petition asking that South Carolina be removed from the "burden they labored under from the Proprietors." In modern English, they wanted the colony taken out of the Proprietors' hands. South Carolina leaders met in a convention that elected James Moore, Jr., to replace Robert Johnson as governor. When Johnson learned of this, he hurried from his plantation and found the militia (nonprofessional local soldiers) beating their drums and ready to proclaim Moore as governor in his place.

"How dare you," Johnson yelled to the militia commander, "to appear in arms [with weapons] against my orders? In the king's name, disperse your men!" The commander answered that he was no longer under Johnson's orders. He was following the orders of the South Carolina convention.

The installation of James Moore, Jr., as governor in late 1719 marked the end of proprietary rule in South Carolina. The convention sent a messenger to England asking that South Carolina be made a royal colony—ruled directly by England's kings and queens instead of by landlords. Royal colonies

King George I of England

could expect more protection, because England's monarchs had a powerful army and navy at their service.

King George I declared South Carolina a royal colony. By 1719 the original Lords Proprietors were dead, and the owners who had replaced them realized that South Carolina wouldn't be very profitable. In 1729, the Proprietors were paid a large sum of money and South Carolina was officially sold to the Crown. That same year, North Carolina also became a royal colony. An interesting sidelight was that the threatened Spanish invasion that prompted South Carolinians to seek royal colony status in 1719 did not take place!

BLACKBEARD (1680?-1718)

Blackbeard was the nickname of one of history's most infamous pirates. His real name is thought to have been Edward Teach, and he may have been born in England or on the British-ruled island of Jamaica, but no one knows for sure. Pirates tried to hide their background so that they couldn't be tracked down through their families. One clue about Teach was that he could read and write, suggesting that he came from a respectable and perhaps even well-to-do family.

Teach first stepped into history during Queen Anne's War (1702–1713), when he worked for England as a privateer out of Jamaica. (Privateers were sailors on armed private ships hired by the government to attack the enemy.) Teach reportedly helped England a great deal by attacking French and Spanish ships during Queen Anne's War. Like many other privateers, Teach turned pirate after the war ended, making his headquarters at the town of Nassau in the Bahama Islands.

Blackbeard

Teach was determined to create a tough "image" for himself. Many pirates drank tremendous amounts of rum in Nassau taverns, but it was said that Teach once mixed his rum with gunpowder, set the concoction on fire, and then drank it! Robbing a large number of ships in a short period of time also enhanced his reputation as a "pirate's pirate."

In about 1717 Teach began robbing ships along what is now the east coast of the United States. Around that time he grew his long black beard, adopted his famous nickname, and began sticking burning matches under his hat before going into battle. All this had a purpose. People started to say that Blackbeard was really the Devil himself. His victims were so scared when they saw him approaching that they often surrendered without a fight.

Now and then, England's monarchs pardoned men who vowed to give up piracy. In early 1718 Blackbeard sailed to Bath, North Carolina, where he promised to become an honest man. He lived for a few months in Bath and even married a sixteen-year-old girl who reportedly was his fourteenth wife! But Blackbeard soon broke his promise and once again began robbing ships. Finally, in late 1718, Virginia's governor Alexander Spotswood sent Robert Maynard to hunt down Blackbeard.

Maynard found Blackbeard along the North Carolina shore. Blackbeard was shot and slashed repeatedly in the battle that followed, yet still fought on. Finally, a British sailor slashed Blackbeard's throat from behind. When Blackbeard's body was examined it was found that it had taken five pistol shots and about twenty sword cuts to finish him off. To prove that Blackbeard was really dead, Maynard cut off the pirate's head and hung it from his ship.

Although Blackbeard was dead, his legend was just beginning. It was said that when Maynard threw Blackbeard's headless body into the water, it swam about for a while before it sank. For many years, when people along the North Carolina coast saw mysterious lights, they claimed that Blackbeard was walking about with a lantern searching for his head. And when howling winds seemed to resemble a human voice, people claimed that it was Blackbeard wailing, "Where is my head?"

Governor Robert Johnson arrives in South Carolina from England,
accompanied by six Cherokee chiefs.

Chapter V

The Colony's Golden Age: 1730-1760s

South Carolina [in the mid-1700s] enjoyed a prosperity that could be matched by few other colonies, if any. . . . Individual Carolinians amassed some of the largest private fortunes in the colonies. . . .

From Colonial South Carolina: A Political History 1663–1763 *by M. Eugene Sirmans*

Robert Johnson, a popular and good governor, had been forced out of office only because he represented the Proprietors. In 1729 Johnson was appointed in England as South Carolina's royal governor. While serving in that position between 1730 and 1735, he did a great deal to improve the colony.

Despite being one of America's wealthiest colonies, South Carolina did have a big problem in Governor Johnson's view. Although a third town—Georgetown—was founded along the Atlantic Ocean in northeastern South Carolina in 1730, the only settled part of South Carolina was still the twenty-mile-wide strip of land along the coast. Johnson helped develop a plan to settle South Carolina's inland regions. Known as "Johnson's township scheme," the plan involved settling colonists from such places as Germany, Switzerland, Ireland, and Wales (the country west of England), as well as English people.

During the 1730s, settlers moved into what are now Orangeburg, Florence, and Society Hill—almost 100 miles inland. One town, established in the 1730s, is not found on the modern map of South Carolina. Called Purrysburgh, it was founded by Jean Pierre Purry of Switzerland, one of the most fascinating characters in South Carolina history.

Purry had the idea that the best climate in the world existed at 33 degrees latitude above the equator and at 33 degrees latitude below the equator. He tried but failed to found colonies in southern Australia and southern Africa in the area of his ideal latitude. Then he decided to found a colony in the New World at about 33 degrees above the equator—a latitude that ran right across South Carolina.

Purry's plan was to send 1,200 French Huguenots who were living in Switzerland to South Carolina, where they would produce large amounts of silk on silkworm farms. About 700 people sent by Purry from Switzerland built Purrysburgh near the Savannah River in southeastern South Carolina. Unfortunately, this was a marshy area, and many of the colonists died of malaria. The survivors gradually moved to healthier regions and Purrysburgh disappeared in the early 1800s.

The people who lived in the outlying settlements in South Carolina were "true" pioneers. They chopped down trees, built log houses, and

This huge live oak grew along the Ashley River. The settlers found ancient forests full of trees in the New World.

Charleston, South Carolina. Map (inset) shows the town in 1732.

survived by growing corn and by hunting and fishing. If they owned slaves, they generally had only one or two rather than the large numbers owned by families in the Charleston area.

While the South Carolina frontier was being settled, Charleston had already become one of America's richest towns. Some planters in the Charleston area owned as many as twelve plantations worked by about 500 slaves. By the mid-1700s, it was becoming popular for families who spent most of the year on their plantations in the countryside to also own a town house in Charleston. Many of these people liked to spend the "social season"—from January to spring-time—in Charleston.

The capital was humming with activity. The colony's first newspaper, the *South Carolina Weekly Journal*, was founded in Charleston by Eleazer Phillips, Jr., around 1730. It lasted just half a year, but in 1732 the *South-Carolina Gazette* appeared, which lasted for over half a century. A publishing "first" was connected with the *Gazette*. In late 1738 its publisher, Lewis Timothy, was killed in an accident. His widow, Elizabeth Timothy, then ran the newspaper for at least a year, becoming the first female newspaper publisher in America. In 1754 a large bookstore was opened in Charleston by Robert Wells, who several years later also began publishing a newspaper called the *South-Carolina Weekly Gazette*.

An important theatrical "first" took place in Charleston on February 12, 1736. That day marked the opening of the Dock Street Theater, America's first true playhouse. The first play performed there was *The Recruiting Officer*, a comedy about army recruiters in England. The original Dock Street Theater is long gone, but a theater of the same name is located where it once stood.

Several other Charleston landmarks were built in the early and mid-1700s. The Old Powder Magazine, a warehouse for storing gunpowder, was built in 1703 and ranks as Charleston's oldest building today. An even more famous Charleston landmark, St. Michael's Episcopal Church, was begun in 1752.

St. Michael's Episcopal Church

In the 1700s rice was already earning many South Carolinians a fortune. In the early 1740s, a young woman developed a second major money-making crop for the colony. Since there were no artificial dyes in colonial times, colors for dyeing cloth had to be obtained from plants. A plant called indigo was used to make a blue dye. Much of the indigo used in England came from France and Spain and was very costly. If indigo could be grown in large quantities in America, it would help the mother country and earn the colonists a great deal of money.

Some South Carolinians had tried to grow indigo without much success. Then around 1739 a South Carolina teenager named Eliza Pinckney began experimenting with growing indigo. After several years of effort, Eliza grew a good indigo

Slaves planting and harvesting indigo

crop in 1744. The news spread, and soon indigo had joined rice as a booming South Carolina farm product. Rice and indigo could be grown effectively on the same plantation. They flourished at different times of year, and while rice grew well on a plantation's lower lands, indigo did well on the higher lands behind the rice paddies. By the late

1740s South Carolina was shipping more than 100,000 pounds of the blue dye to England each year. The crop helped make many planters rich, and South Carolina enjoyed a golden age that lasted until the end of colonial times.

But the colony that was a land of opportunity for white colonists was a place of drudgery and hopelessness for the black slaves. The colonists' worst nightmare was that the slaves would revolt, which happened from time to time. Usually the plans were discovered and the revolt was squashed before it could get very far, but a huge slave rebellion occurred in 1739.

Relations between England and Spain were very bad by the late 1730s. In 1738 the Spanish issued a proclamation intended to hurt England's southern colonies. Slaves who escaped to Florida would be freed by the Spanish. The Spaniards even maintained a camp called Fort Moosa outside St. Augustine for the escaped slaves. Naturally, planters did not want their slaves to learn of the Spaniards' offer, but the news spread from plantation to plantation. By mid-1739 a number of South Carolina slaves had escaped to Florida, and others hoped to join them.

Three factors convinced some South Carolina slaves that a Sunday in early September of 1739 was the perfect time to revolt. First, the colony was weaker than usual because of a yellow fever epidemic late that summer that had killed many people in the Charleston area. Second, on or around Saturday, September 8, 1739, word reached South Carolina that England and Spain had begun fighting over shipping at sea. This war began after the Spaniards reportedly sliced off the ear of an English sea captain named Robert Jenkins, and became known as the War of Jenkins' Ear. The slaves knew that the colonists would be preoccupied with the outbreak of the war rather than a possible slave revolt. What made a Sunday ideal was that many white males attended church services without weapons.

Early on the morning of Sunday, September 9, 1739, about twenty slaves attacked a store along the Stono River a few miles southwest of Charleston. It is thought that the slaves were led by a man named Jemmy or Jonny. The slaves killed the two storekeepers, seized some guns and powder, and went out to wage war on the white people of the area.

The slaves traveled from house to house killing men, women, and children. They spared at least one man, an innkeeper who reportedly "was a good man and kind to his slaves." The rebels planned to march south through Georgia all the way down to St. Augustine, Florida. As they headed down the road shouting "Liberty!" and beating drums, they were joined by more slaves.

By chance, Governor William Bull was riding in the opposite direction to Charleston at that very time. Governor Bull's path crossed that of the approximately fifty rebels at eleven o'clock in the morning. If Bull hadn't wheeled about and ridden away, he probably would have been captured and killed, which would have caused widespread panic in South Carolina. The slaves may not have known that the man who barely eluded them was the governor.

By Sunday afternoon the slaves had gone only about ten miles and were still in South Carolina. They decided to rest for a while in a field near the road, perhaps hoping that other slaves would learn they were there and join them. Meanwhile, a number of white men had learned of the revolt, perhaps from Governor Bull. At about four o'clock in the afternoon, some fifty white planters carrying guns approached the slaves on horseback. Some of the slaves fled, but others held their ground and fought. At least fourteen slaves who survived the fight were captured and then shot. Reportedly the planters cut off the heads of some of the dead slaves and set them on posts along the road.

It took a few more weeks for the planters to track down most of the remaining rebels, who were then shot, hanged, or tortured to death. By the time the Stono Rebellion had been completely crushed in the spring of 1740, thirty whites and perhaps twice as many slaves had been killed, making it one of the deadliest slave revolts of colonial times.

After the Stono Rebellion ended, South Carolina men were ordered to carry guns to church. Stricter slave laws were passed, too.

According to the slave code of 1740, slaves were forbidden to hold their own meetings, and selling alcohol to slaves—or even teaching them to write—were made crimes. The code banned the teaching of writing because slave revolts in colonial America were often led by educated blacks.

South Carolinians placed laws in the 1740 code that were supposed to benefit the slaves. It was made illegal to work slaves more than fifteen hours per day between March 25 and September 25, or more than fourteen hours a day in other seasons. Slaves were to have Sundays off. It was also made a crime for a master to kill a slave, punishable by a stiff fine. Today, assuring people of "only" a ninety-hour workweek and making it possible for a murderer to pay for the crime with money seems very wrong. Yet the South Carolina lawmakers of 1740 felt they were being humane because they had the power to deny the slaves any rights at all. But the lawmakers weren't trying to protect the slaves just out of a sense of justice. They realized that extremely cruel masters could bring on another slave revolt. For the most part, the 1740 slave code worked as intended. There were minor uprisings, but no more major slave rebellions in South Carolina for the rest of the colonial era.

However, there were plenty of threats from England's two old enemies—Spain and France. Ever since 1565, Spain had held Florida, to the south of England's thirteen colonies. And since the early 1600s, France had ruled part of Canada, which it called New France, to the north of the thirteen colonies. England, France, and Spain had their eyes on one another's North American lands. Between the late 1600s and 1763 the three nations fought several wars for control of North America. These "Colonial Wars" were part of a larger struggle on land and sea to determine which nation would become the strongest power on earth.

The War of Jenkins' Ear (1739-1744), which began about the time the Stono Rebellion broke out, threatened South Carolina's very existence. For a time during this war it appeared that Spain might seize Georgia and both Carolinas. In 1740 Georgia governor James Oglethorpe tried to end the threat from Spain by seizing St. Augustine. About 400 South Carolinians joined this expedition, which was a total failure. However, in

James Oglethorpe

Oglethorpe's expedition against the Spanish at St. Augustine, Florida failed.

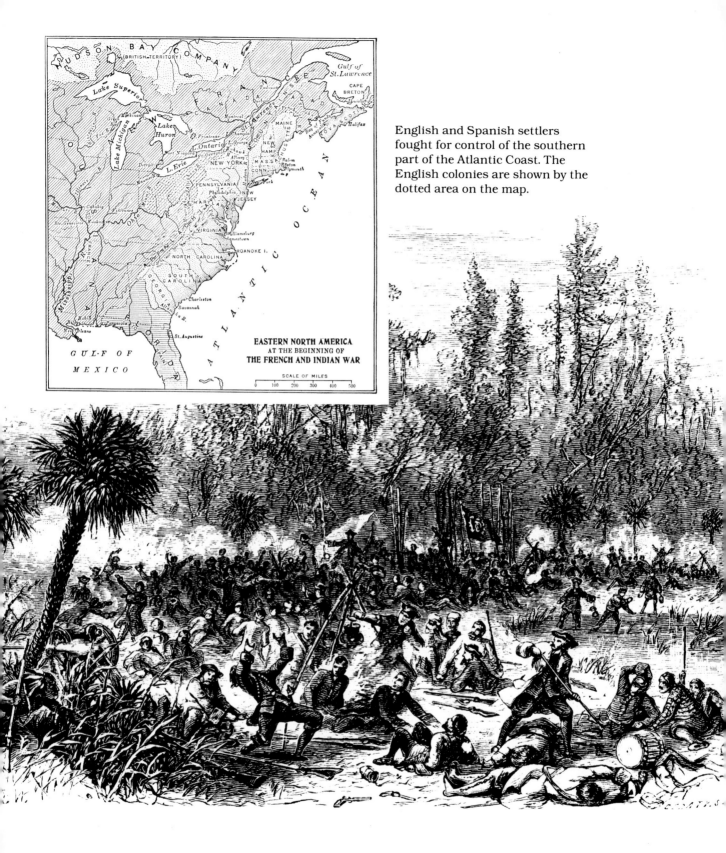

English and Spanish settlers fought for control of the southern part of the Atlantic Coast. The English colonies are shown by the dotted area on the map.

EASTERN NORTH AMERICA
AT THE BEGINNING OF
THE FRENCH AND INDIAN WAR

SCALE OF MILES
0   100   200   300   400   500

the summer of 1742 Oglethorpe's forces crushed the Spaniards at the Battle of Bloody Marsh in Georgia. Two years later, the War of Jenkins' Ear ended with England still in control of Georgia and the Carolinas.

Between 1689 and 1763 England and France fought four wars for control of North America. The issue wasn't decided until the fourth and last of these clashes, the French and Indian War (1754–1763), in which thousands of Native Americans helped the French fight English and American troops. No major battles occurred in South Carolina, but hundreds of South Carolinians helped English forces win the French and Indian War. With this victory, England emerged as the dominant force in North America. Few people could have dreamed that the English would soon be fighting the very people who had helped them defeat France—the American colonists.

ELIZA LUCAS PINCKNEY (1722–1793)

Elizabeth Lucas, or Eliza as she was called, was probably born on the British-ruled island of Antigua in the West Indies, where her father was an officer in the English army. As a child, Eliza sailed to England for her education. Few boys of her time—and only a handful of girls—were as well educated as Eliza. We know this from the many interesting letters and notes she wrote, starting when she was still a teenager.

Eliza was about fifteen when she moved with her family to South Carolina for the sake of her mother's health. The family settled at a plantation called Wappoo, not far from Charleston. They had lived there only a short time when Eliza's father was called back to Antigua, where he became royal governor. Although Eliza was just sixteen, her father placed her in charge of his three plantations and his business dealings in his absence. He knew that she was more grown-up and capable than many people twice her age.

Awakening each day at 5 A.M., Eliza managed her father's affairs and did a great deal more besides. She ran a school for her family's young slaves. She also spent many hours on her hobbies—reading, music lessons, and gardening. "I love the vegetable world extremely," Eliza wrote to a friend in Charleston. She loved experimenting to see which crops grew well in South Carolina. Eliza first tried to grow indigo when her father had been away just a short time. At first she failed, but she kept trying, and by 1744 Eliza was producing indigo successfully. She taught her neighbors to grow the plant, and soon indigo was a leading money-maker for South Carolinians. This remarkable young woman also helped her neighbors in another way. She studied law on her own and began drawing up wills for people she knew.

Several neighbors who knew that Eliza's father was away and that her mother was ill took the young woman under their wing. Two of them—a mother and daughter—were descendants of Dr. Henry Woodward, South Carolina's first English resident. Eliza herself described how another neighbor worried about her. This elderly woman was afraid that Eliza would "read myself mad," and that her habit of awakening so early would "spoil my marriage, for she says it will make me look old long before I am so."

In those days, fathers often suggested a suitable husband for their daughters. Governor Lucas wrote Eliza urging that she marry one of two gentlemen. Her response was that she wouldn't marry "Mr. L." for all "the riches of Chile and Peru together if he had them." As for the other man, she explained that she couldn't marry someone she barely knew.

Eighteen-year-old Eliza made it clear to her father that when the time came she would choose her own husband.

A childless couple named Colonel Charles Pinckney and Elizabeth Lamb Pinckney were two of Eliza's closest friends. Eliza often visited their home, where she borrowed books from the colonel, a rich planter and lawyer. It was said that Mrs. Pinckney, whose health was poor, made it known that in the event of her death she hoped her husband would marry Eliza. Mrs. Pinckney died in early 1744. Four months later, around the time of her triumph with indigo, twenty-two-year-old Eliza married Charles Pinckney.

Eliza Lucas Pinckney went to live at Belmont, her husband's beautiful plantation, just a few miles outside Charleston. From there, she continued to take care of her father's affairs. Eliza also experimented with growing flax and hemp, and with producing silk. Dr. Alexander Garden befriended Eliza and helped her with some of her plant experiments.

Eliza was good at raising children as well as plants. She and her husband had three children who lived to adulthood—Charles Cotesworth, Harriott, and Thomas Pinckney. Eliza and her husband were ahead of their time in their feeling that children could learn at a much younger age than was generally believed. When their oldest child, Charles Cotesworth, was only a few months old, they made him a set of spelling blocks. A short time later, Eliza bragged in a letter to her sister, "He can tell all his letters in any book without hesitation, and begins to spell before he is two years old."

When Eliza was thirty-six, her husband died. She then took over his affairs, just as she had for her father twenty years earlier. She spent the second half of her life managing her plantations and helping to raise some of her grandchildren. Eliza Lucas Pinckney, who had begun South Carolina's indigo industry half a century earlier, died at the age of seventy-one in Philadelphia, where she had gone for cancer treatment. Eliza's sons Charles Cotesworth Pinckney and Thomas Pinckney both became famous statesmen.

Chapter VI

Life in South Carolina in the 1760s

The merchants of Charleston were prospering from trade with London [and with other cities in Great Britain]. The rice planters were getting richer from abundant crops shipped overseas. . . . Indigo, thanks to a bounty paid by the British government for every pound produced in the colonies, was bringing in additional revenue. . . . The back country was filling up rapidly with immigrants. . . . In short, South Carolinians in 1763 . . . were as content as human beings are likely to be in this imperfect world.

From South Carolina: A Bicentennial History *by Louis B. Wright*

If we could go back in time to colonial America, something about the people might seem strange to us. There weren't very many of them! The thirteen colonies in 1760 were home to only about 1.5 million settlers and slaves—about 1/150th of the U.S. population today. New York City alone now has about five times as many people as lived in all thirteen colonies in 1760. About 100,000 of those 1.5 million people lived in South Carolina. Some football and baseball games attract almost

A Carolina rice field. Rice grew well in the wetlands of South Carolina.

that many people today, yet South Carolina's population was close to average among the thirteen colonies for the year 1760.

South Carolina had plenty of human variety. About 60,000 of its 100,000 inhabitants were black. A little more than half of the white people were of English origin, while the rest were of Scottish, Irish, German, French, and other backgrounds. One test of a colony's openness to minorities is how it treated Jewish people, a group that was persecuted throughout much of the world. South Carolina was one of only a few colonies where Jews were welcome. By 1749 there were enough Jews in Charleston to form a congregation—Kahal Kadosh Beth Elohim (Holy

Congregation House of God)—which today is one of the oldest ongoing Jewish congregations in the United States.

South Carolinians of the 1760s thought of their colony as having two regions. They called the sixty-mile strip along the Atlantic Ocean the Low Country. The colony's most important towns—Charleston, Georgetown, and Beaufort—were in the Low Country. The rest of South Carolina was called the Up Country or Backcountry. By the 1760s much of the Up Country was settled. For example, the town of Winnsboro not far from the center of South Carolina was settled about 1755, and the first settler in the Greenville region in western South Carolina arrived about ten years later. Many of the Up Country settlers had moved there from such colonies as Pennsylvania, Maryland, and Virginia. Other people had sailed from Europe to Charleston before moving inland to the South Carolina frontier. It is believed that by the mid-1760s as much as three-fourths of South Carolina's white population lived in the Up Country.

South Carolina was famous throughout America as one of the richest of the thirteen colonies. In 1763, Dr. George Milligen Johnston

The wealthy planters lived in mansions like these. Slaves did all the work in their fields and homes.

wrote a book called *A Short Description of the Province of South-Carolina*, which he updated a few years later. The doctor wrote that in late colonial times South Carolina was not only the wealthiest American colony but "the most thriving Country perhaps on this Globe."

Most of the richest South Carolinians lived in the Low Country, where nearly all of the colony's large plantations were located. The wealthiest planters owned dozens or even hundreds of slaves. Even the "poorer" Low Country farmers generally owned two or three slaves.

House servant

A typical Low Country planter might devote several hours a day to business. The rest of the time, he and his family enjoyed such leisure activities as reading and socializing. Slaves attended to the family's every need. Field slaves grew the rice and indigo that made the planters rich. House slaves dressed them in their lovely clothes, wigs, and jewels, and cooked them such delicious foods as calapash (turtle cooked in the shell) and shrimp and rice dishes. Slaves also drove them to neighboring plantations and to Charleston in the family carriage.

A smartly dressed planter's wife alights from the family coach.

View of the city of Charleston, South Carolina, in 1762

By 1760 Charleston was the richest town in the thirteen colonies. Planters for many miles around sent rice, indigo, and other goods by wagon to Charleston over the Low Country's fine roads. In Charleston these products were bought by merchants and shipped to many distant places. For a town of about 10,000 people, Charleston had an incredibly busy port. At any given time, there might be 100 ships loading or unloading goods in Charleston Harbor.

Charleston was also the social center for the rich and famous South Carolinians. The big news in the Charleston theater world in the spring of 1764 was that the famous star "Miss Cheer" was appearing in a play called *A Wonder! A Woman Keeps a Secret!* Two popular plays of 1766 were *The Orphan of China* and *The School for Lovers.* Musical concerts were well attended, and in 1762, America's first musical club, the St. Cecilia Society, was founded in Charleston. For those who like a little more action, horse races were held at the New Market Course just outside Charleston, starting in the early 1760s.

According to a joke of the time, wealthy men could be found anywhere but at home during Charleston's "social season," which lasted from January into the spring. If they weren't at the race track or at one of the town's approximately 100 "tippling houses" (taverns), they might be at a club. Charlestonians were "club happy." Various groups such as the English, the Scots, and the Germans had their own clubs, some of which were founded to provide help for newcomers to the colony. There were also a number of clubs in Charleston where men passed the time in amusing ways. The Candlestick Club boasted that it met in a different tavern every night. There was even a club in Charleston that was devoted to eating beefsteak, and another that was dedicated to laughing!

Since Charleston was the capital of South Carolina, the governor, who had been appointed by the king, lived there, and the legislature met there. Many Americans today have the mistaken notion that in colonial times poor people had a better chance to succeed in politics than they do today. The truth is that in colonial days poor people, blacks, and women couldn't even vote, let alone hold office, and nearly all elected officials were rich—or at least rather well-off—white men. Most of the members of the two houses of South Carolina's legislature—the Council and the Commons House of Assembly—were Low Country planters, merchants, and lawyers.

The prominent Low Country families were related to each other in all kinds of interesting ways. Eliza Lucas Pinckney's family tree, for example, had many famous people on its branches. Eliza's son Charles Cotesworth Pinckney married Sarah Middleton, daughter of Continental Congress president Henry Middleton. Eliza's daughter, Harriott Pinckney, married Daniel Horry, one of the richest planters along South Carolina's Santee River. And Eliza's son

Thomas Pinckney

Charles Pinckney

Thomas Pinckney married Elizabeth Motte, a granddaughter of South Carolina treasurer Jacob Motte. Eliza was also related by marriage to Charles Pinckney, a famous governor of South Carolina. Charles Pinckney's wife, Mary Eleanor, was the daughter of Henry Laurens, another South Carolinian who served as president of the Continental Congress. Prominent South Carolinians had so many ties by blood and marriage that the colony could almost be said to have been run by one big family of Low Country people.

South Carolina's 60,000 slaves, most of whom lived in the Low Country, had a totally different kind of existence than their masters. Either they or their ancestors had been brought from Africa in slave ships. The slaves were chained up in spaces about the size of a coffin during the ocean crossing. Once each day the captain and crew paraded the slaves on deck and made them jump around by cracking their whips at them. It was hoped that this exercise would keep the slaves healthy, but about one-fifth of them died of disease on the voyage to America and were buried at sea. Sometimes slaves who were very sick, but still living, were thrown into the water to drown, so that they wouldn't infect the other slaves.

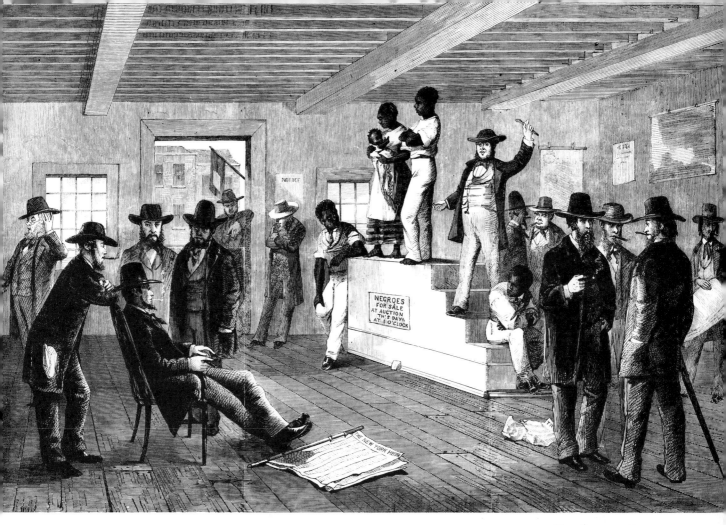

At a slave auction, fathers, mothers, and their children might be sold to separate owners and parted forever.

Charleston was the main port of entry for slaves in the thirteen colonies. Nearly half of all the slaves shipped to the colonies between 1700 and 1775 arrived at Charleston. Slaves were sold to the highest bidders at auctions, which in Charleston were attended by people from other colonies besides South Carolina. The cries and shrieks of the black people made the slave auctions pitiful for anyone who had a heart.

Besides losing their freedom, the slaves knew that they might never see their family again. The father might be sold to a North Carolinian, the mother to a Virginian, and the children to a South Carolinian.

Some masters let their slaves keep their African names, such as Quame, Phiba, Mimba, and Cuffee. Others gave their slaves common English names, such as Jack, George, Esther, Sue, and Phyllis. Still other masters gave their slaves fancy names such as Christmas, Friday, Hercules, Juno, and London. The slaves had no last names. Just as cowboys brand their cattle, some masters branded their slaves on the chest or another part of the body. If the slaves ever ran away and were captured, they could be identified by this brand.

Once at their new home, the slaves were put to work. Few Americans today work as hard as the slaves did. Many of them spent their days growing and harvesting rice, indigo, and other crops. At times of the year when there was little farm work, many masters hired out their slaves to work in Charleston and other towns as fishermen, carpenters, garbage collectors, stevedores (people who load and unload ships), and porters (people who carry things for others). In most cases, all the

TO BE SOLD by William Yeomans, (in Charles Town Merchant,) a parcel of good Plantation Slaves. Encouragement will be given by taking Rice in Payment, or any Saddles and Furniture, choice Barbados and Boston Rum, also Cordial Waters and Limejuice, as well as a parcel of extraordinary Indian trading Goods, and many of other sorts suitable for the Season.

An ad announcing
a slave sale

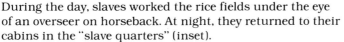

During the day, slaves worked the rice fields under the eye of an overseer on horseback. At night, they returned to their cabins in the "slave quarters" (inset).

money the slaves earned was handed over to their masters.

The slaves usually lived in the "slave quarters," which were often rows of small huts at some distance from the planter's big house. Many masters spent as little money as they could on their slaves' needs. They fed them meat fat, skimmed milk, and moldy bacon, and gave them a minimum of clothing. In South Carolina and other colonies with a warm climate, some slaves weren't given any clothing at all until they were about thirteen years old.

White men regularly patrolled the slave quarters to see that no weapons were being stocked or rebellions planned. These men, whom the slaves called "patrollers" or "pattyrollers," often abused their power. Instead of punishing only slaves who broke the rules, some went out and "beat up quarters," meaning that they assaulted every slave they saw.

Hundreds of slaves tried to escape from their masters, as proven by the advertisements for runaway slaves that appeared in South Carolina newspapers. Slave children as young as twelve years old were known to run away. If captured, the slaves might be tied to a tree and whipped viciously. Slaves who attacked their masters or who were thought to be planning a revolt were sometimes executed.

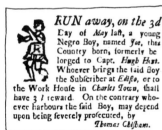

Ad for a runaway slave

Nearly all of the written descriptions of slavery in colonial times were provided by white people, because few slaves could read or write. However, after the slaves were freed in the 1860s, some of them told or wrote down descriptions of their lives in slavery. Here are a few such descriptions by former South Carolina slaves. Although they were made long after colonial times, these descriptions would hold true for the 1760s:

Want to know how they [the slave children] were fed? Well, it was like this. You've seen pig troughs, side by side, in a big lot? After all the grown slaves ate and got out of the way, scraps and everything eatable were put in some troughs. Sometimes buttermilk was poured in the mess . . . then the cook blowed a cow horn. Quick as lightning a passel of 50 or 60 children ran out of the plum bushes, from under the sheds and houses, and from everywhere. Each one took his place and soused his hands in the mixture and ate just like you see pigs shoving around slop troughs.

I was small in slavery times, and played with the white chaps. Once he [the master] saw me and some other chaps, white chaps, under a tree playing with letter blocks. They had the ABCs on them. Master got awful mad and got off his horse and whipped me good.

My master was good to all his slaves, but Missy [the master's wife] was mean to us. She whipped us a heap of times when we ain't done nothing bad to be whipped for. When she went to whip me, she tied my wrists together with a rope and put that rope through a big staple in the ceiling and drew me up off the floor and gave me a hundred lashes. I think about my old mammy [mother] heap of times now and how I've seen her whipped, with the blood dripping off of her. All that us slaves knew how to do was to work hard. We never learned to read and write. Nor we never had no church to go to, only sometimes the white folks let us go to their church, but we never joined in the singing. We just sat and listened to them preach and pray.

Like all the other colonies, South Carolina was also home to some very poor white people.

Making horseshoe
nails by hand

According to James Glen, who governed South Carolina in the mid-1700s, one-fifth of all white South Carolinians had "a bare subsistence," meaning that they had trouble getting enough to eat. Charleston had many beggars and prostitutes (women who engage in sex for money) who lived in poverty. The colony made some provisions for its poor. For example, in the late 1750s a doctor and scientist named Alexander Garden was hired to care for the poor people of Charleston. Garden treated many poor people during a severe small-pox epidemic that killed hundreds of Charleston-ians in 1760. The Up Country was home to numerous drifters whom we would call "homeless people" today. These people often slept outdoors as they moved around the region struggling to find food. Of course, there was one great difference between the black slaves and the poor white South Carolinians. The slaves had no choice about how they lived.

Between the rich white plantation owners at the top of the social ladder and the black slaves and poor whites at the bottom were thousands of what we might call middle-class families. They included white shopkeepers in Charleston and the other towns, and also such people as ministers, teachers, and tailors. South Carolina

Up Country settlers cleared the land and built log cabins.

was also home to several hundred free black people in the 1760s, many of whom had been liberated by the terms of their masters' wills. A few of the free blacks owned plantations and slaves of their own, but most of them earned a living as fishermen and carpenters, and worked at other jobs that slaves were hired out to do. However, the free blacks could keep their wages and, most important of all, they had their liberty.

Making wooden shingles

The majority of middle-class people were Up Country farmers. Unlike the Low Country planters, the Up Country families generally did their own work without the help of slaves. They cleared their land of trees and used the wood to build their cabins. They also made their own tables, chairs, beds, and even dishes and spoons out of wood. Frontier people saved animal fat and made it into candles, and used fat and fireplace ashes to make soap. The women sewed the family's clothes out of deerskin or homemade cloth, except for perhaps one set of Sunday clothes bought in Charleston.

Up Country settler

Mealtime was quite different for the frontier families than it was for the rich planters. Many of them may have had nightmares about corn because they ate it—and even drank it—so often in the form of corn bread, succotash (corn and beans mixed together), corn stews, and corn beer. Nearly every backwoodsman also hunted. If he was lucky and a good shot, his family might have venison (deer meat) or a rabbit or squirrel stew for dinner.

The farther from town the colonists lived, the less likely they were to have contact with ministers or teachers. Many couples lived together and had children without being formally married because there was no minister around to perform the ceremony. One minister who worked in South Carolina in the mid-1700s wrote a letter complaining that among the couples he had married over the past year, nearly all of the brides had been pregnant.

There were a few schools on the frontier. For example, a boy named Andrew Jackson who was born on the South Carolina-North Carolina border (probably on the South Carolina side) attended a church school that helped prepare him for his later role as the seventh president of the United States. But many frontier children never saw the inside of a schoolhouse. Their only education came from their parents—if *they* knew how to read and write.

Although they didn't attend balls or the theater, the frontier people knew how to have fun too. They held "frolics" at which they danced to the tune of a fiddle, and held "house-raisings" to help new families put up their cabins. Once the home was finished, everyone took part in the dancing and shooting and wrestling contests.

The frontier people were angry at the Low Country people over one big issue. Even though they made up as much as three-fourths of South Carolina's white population, Up Country people were allowed very few representatives in the colonial legislature at Charleston, which was run by Low Countrymen. But by and large, life was going well for most Up Country colonists in the 1760s. In 1760–61 the Cherokee, who were struggling to retain their lands, were defeated by the colonists in important battles in the western parts of both Carolinas. In 1761 the Cherokee made a peace treaty with the colonists that granted large western portions of Virginia and North and South Carolina to the American settlers. Life was so good for most white South Carolinians in the 1760s that they would have been content to remain under English rule for many more years—if England hadn't begun making certain demands.

DR. ALEXANDER GARDEN (1730-1791)

Nearly everyone has seen or at least heard of the lovely white flower called the gardenia, but few people know that it was named for Alexander Garden, a doctor and scientist who lived in South Carolina more than two hundred years ago. The son of a minister, Alexander was born in Scotland. He attended school in his hometown, and by the age of sixteen had decided to become a doctor. Alexander worked for a time as a surgeon's helper on British ships, and also studied medicine at universities in Scotland. About the time that he earned his M.D., he was invited to become the partner of a doctor who lived near Charleston, South Carolina. Alexander said good-bye to his family and sailed to Charleston in the spring of 1752.

Garden built up a very successful medical practice, often working from seven o'clock in the morning until nine at night. Among his prominent patients and friends were Eliza Pinckney, Henry and John Laurens, and Henry Middleton. He also helped care for Charleston's poor people. On Christmas Day in 1755, Dr. Garden married a South Carolina girl—Elizabeth Peronneau—with whom he raised three children.

Despite his hectic schedule, Alexander Garden found time for a hobby. In colonial days, many living things that were native to America were unknown to European scientists. Alexander walked about the countryside collecting samples of plants and animals. He even visited fishermen's homes to see if they had caught anything unusual, and was known to snatch their fish dinners off their tables to obtain specimens! Garden sent some of his specimens to such famous scientists as Sweden's Carolus Linnaeus, who founded the modern method of giving two-part scientific names to plants and animals.

While out collecting, Dr. Garden made a number of discoveries, including the two-toed Congo eel and the mud iguana. He was also one of the first scientists to describe the powers of pinkroot, a plant that was used as a medicine for destroying worms in the human intestine.

During the mid-1700s something happened thousands of miles from South Carolina that made Alexander Garden's name a household word. In South Africa, a British sea captain found a beautiful white flower with a wonderful fragrance. He packed the flower in soil and brought it to England, where he gave it to a friend named Richard Warner. Scientists determined that the flower was previously unknown. Some people wanted to call it Warneria, for the man who first grew it in England, while others wanted to call it Augusta or Portlandia. But in 1760 Carolus Linnaeus named it the gardenia, for Dr. Alexander Garden. Scientists in those days were sometimes honored by having newly discovered living things named for them, even if they hadn't been involved in the discovery.

Dr. Garden expected to live out his days in South Carolina, but the Revolutionary War prevented that. Garden was loyal to England. When the American patriots won the war, they punished Loyalists such as Dr. Garden by seizing their belongings. In 1782 South Carolina officials began seizing Garden's property. Later that year, along with his wife and their nine-year-old daughter, Dr. Garden sailed to England. Dr. Garden's health had been ruined by years of working eighteen-hour days, and he died in England at the age of sixty-one. His property was restored to his son, Major Alexander Garden, who fought on the patriot side in the Revolutionary War against his father's wishes. The beautiful gardenia—the flower named for Dr. Alexander Garden—is now grown in many places throughout the world.

Signing the Declaration of Independence, July 4, 1776

Chapter VII

The Revolutionary War

AUT MORS AUT LIBERTAS [Latin, meaning EITHER DEATH OR LIBERTY]

> *From a newspaper article by Christopher Gadsden that appeared in 1766*

There was good news and bad news for the American colonists after they helped England win the French and Indian War in 1763. The good news was that the American colonists were no longer threatened by the French, and that the Native Americans were less of a danger. The bad news was that England was deeply in debt, partly due to the cost of the war. The British lawmaking body, called Parliament, decided that since the Americans had gained by the French and Indian War, they should pay taxes to help settle the mother country's debt.

People in America were shocked by this development. Most of them felt that they should be thanked for their efforts in the French and Indian War, not told to pay taxes. Some English

Tax stamp

Handbill of the True
Sons of Liberty

lawmakers warned Parliament that the Americans might fight over the taxes, but they were in the minority. Between 1764 and 1773, Parliament taxed the Americans on many items ranging from newspapers to tea.

The Stamp Act of 1765, a tax on papers and documents that were used in everyday life, was the first new tax to deeply anger the colonists. Starting November 1, 1765, special stamps were to be bought and affixed to all newspapers, wills, and various other papers. From Georgia to Maine, Americans cried that "Taxation without representation is tyranny!" meaning that since they weren't allowed to send representatives to Parliament, the British government had no right to tax them. In the months before the new law was scheduled to take effect, the colonists protested the Stamp Act in speeches, newspaper articles, meetings, and even riots.

The most violent protests occurred in Boston, Massachusetts, where men calling themselves the Sons of Liberty burned and smashed buildings belonging to British officials. Other colonies also formed groups called the Sons of Liberty or the Liberty Boys. Led by Christopher Gadsden among others, Charleston's Sons of Liberty sometimes met beneath a huge oak known as the Liberty

Tree, where they gave angry speeches against British injustice.

On October 18, 1765, the ship *Planters Adventure* arrived at Fort Johnson in Charleston Harbor carrying stamps intended for sale in South Carolina. The Sons of Liberty were determined that the stamps wouldn't be used when the law took effect two weeks later. They built a gallows (a device on which criminals are hanged), complete with a dummy made to look like a hanged British stamp official. The British officials understood the message. If they distributed the stamps, *they* might be hanging on the gallows the next time! A mob made up partly of Sons of Liberty also went around Charleston searching for the hidden stamps. The mob found two Stamp Act officials and pressured them into quitting their posts.

The American patriots knew that a united thirteen colonies would be stronger than all of the colonies acting separately. The same month that the protests took place in Charleston, delegates from nine colonies including South Carolina met in New York City to plan a unified response to the Stamp Act. Christopher Gadsden, John Rutledge, and Thomas Lynch were South Carolina's delegates. At this meeting Gadsden made a speech in

Stamp officials were hung in effigy

Christopher Gadsden

which he said that Americans should start viewing themselves as one people. "There ought to be no New England man, no New Yorker, known on the continent, but all of us Americans," Gadsden said. The Stamp Act Congress sent a message to British lawmakers that Americans would not "be taxed without their consent."

When November 1 arrived, Britain found it impossible to enforce the Stamp Act. South Carolinians and colonists elsewhere played a trick on the British on that day after Halloween in 1765. They closed courts and offices rather than use the hated tax stamps. Only in Georgia were stamps sold, and not many were sold there. Realizing that it was a failure, British lawmakers repealed the Stamp Act in March 1766. The Americans had won the first round, but the British still expected to win the fight.

In 1767 Parliament passed the Townshend Acts, which taxed certain goods, including paint and tea, that were brought into the colonies. Large numbers of Americans struck back at the British where it hurt the most—in their wallets—by refusing to buy British goods. For example, instead of buying British-made clothing, they wore homespun garments. When they did buy goods from abroad, they bought them from non-

Woman spinning to avoid buying English cloth

British nations. Seeing that the Townshend Acts weren't working, Parliament repealed all of them in 1770, except the tax on tea. The desire for money wasn't the only reason Britain kept this one last Townshend tax.

Have you ever seen an argument in which a disobedient child makes a parent angrier and angrier? The quarrel between Britain and America was a lot like this by 1770. England was even called the "mother country" because it ruled the thirteen colonies and most of the colonists were of English ancestry. Most people in England viewed the Americans as wayward children who must be taught to obey. The Americans, on the other hand, felt that the English were pushing them around and taking advantage of the fact that their country was older and stronger.

Sometimes in an argument a parent comes up with a clever way to get the child to obey. English lawmakers did this—or so they thought. In 1773 Parliament passed a new law called the Tea Act, which kept the tax on tea but lowered the price, making it cheaper than non-English tea. The English expected that the Americans would run out to buy the tea because of its overall lower price, and that they wouldn't care about the tax. This would show the world that saving money meant more to the Americans than the "taxation without representation" issue.

Instead of taking the bait, thousands of women brewed "liberty tea" out of sassafras bark, or even catnip, for their families. And some patriots decided that the British tea should be drunk—but only by fish in the ocean!

As with the Stamp Act, Massachusetts led the fight against the Tea Act. On December 16, 1773, about 50 Bostonians dumped 340 chests of English tea into Boston Harbor. The British

Patriots dressed up as Indians dumped tea into the harbor at the Boston Tea Party.

punished the people of the Massachusetts capital for their Boston Tea Party. For one thing, they closed the port of Boston on June 1, 1774, causing great hardship in the town. Hundreds of Bostonians involved in shipping were suddenly out of work, and the town also suffered a food shortage.

The British hoped that colonists elsewhere would not help the Bostonians, but there was a growing feeling in America that "an attack upon the liberties of one Colony is an attack upon the liberties of all," as Samuel Adams, the organizer of the Boston Tea Party, expressed it. Food from other colonies poured into Boston. In many cases it was shipped to nearby towns, then taken by cart overland into Boston. South Carolinians contributed a large quantity of their best-known food product—rice. The Boston Tea Party also inspired less-famous tea parties in New York, Maryland, New Jersey, and both Carolinas. South Carolinians threw a shipload of tea into Charleston Harbor on November 1, 1774.

American leaders decided to meet as they had during the Stamp Act crisis to fight the Tea Act and other British measures such as the Boston port closing. From September 5 to October 26, 1774, a meeting of colonial leaders was held in Philadelphia, Pennsylvania. Every colony but

Samuel Adams

Patrick Henry

John Hancock

Georgia sent delegates to this First Continental Congress. South Carolina's delegates were Christopher Gadsden, the brothers John and Edward Rutledge, Thomas Lynch, and Henry Middleton.

The First Continental Congress was the seed from which the United States Congress later grew, but no one knew that then. Only a few delegates including Christopher Gadsden, Patrick Henry of Virginia, and Samuel Adams of Massachusetts were seriously thinking about independence as yet. The majority only sought fairer treatment for America. The First Continental Congress sent letters to England asking that it end the taxation and the punishment of Boston for its Tea Party, but Congress also told the colonies to prepare their militias in case of war with England. Congress planned to meet again in the spring of 1775 if Britain wouldn't yield. The mother country not only stuck to its guns, it began firing them.

On the night of April 18, 1775, British troops stationed in Boston, Massachusetts, secretly left the city. The redcoats, as the Americans called the British soldiers, were on a double mission. First they were to arrest Samuel Adams and John Hancock, who were hiding in Lexington, Massachusetts, a few miles outside Boston. The British hoped that once these two rebel leaders were out of the way, other Americans would calm down. After arresting Adams and Hancock, the redcoats planned to seize military supplies that the rebels had stored in nearby Concord, Massachusetts.

American patriots in Boston learned of the British plans and sent Paul Revere to warn Adams and Hancock that the redcoats were coming. Revere made the most famous ride in American history on the night of April 18, 1775. Thanks to Revere's warning, Adams and Hancock escaped

Paul Revere warning the people of Lexington that the British are coming

The "first blow for liberty" was struck at the Battle of Lexington.

Lexington while the town's militiamen hurried to the village green to meet the redcoats. At dawn of April 19, 1775, about seventy-five Lexington militiamen fought a larger number of redcoats who had entered their town. The British easily won the Battle of Lexington. Only one redcoat was wounded while eight Americans were killed and ten were wounded in this opening battle of the Revolutionary War (1775–1783).

Later that same day, Massachusetts militiamen and redcoats clashed again at nearby Concord. This time the Americans outnumbered the redcoats, and they were also in a rage over the defeat at Lexington. The patriots defeated the redcoats at Concord's North Bridge, then chased them back toward Boston, shooting at them along the way. Nearly 300 of the retreating redcoats were killed or wounded in the running Battle of Concord, compared with about 100 American losses.

The Minutemen were patriot farmers ready to fight at a minute's notice

In January 1775, South Carolinians had formed a new government called the Provincial Congress. It proved to be a temporary legislature in the transition from the colonial British government to the state government that would be created in 1776. News traveled at such a snail's pace in those days that the Provincial Congress in Charleston didn't know for about three weeks what had happened 1,000 miles to the north at Lexington and Concord. After learning of these battles, the Provincial Congress raised troops to fight the English if necessary, and its members signed a paper pledging that they were "ready to sacrifice our lives and fortunes" for the American cause.

Nearly everyone in America was extremely worried and confused over the next few months.

Some Americans felt that the battles of Lexington and Concord would convince Britain to back down and give in to their demands. The colonists could then return to English rule, but with much more freedom. Other people were ready to fight an all-out war to obtain justice from England. Still others were terrified that England, the world's strongest nation, would crush them in a war and then take revenge upon them. And some colonists who were loyal to England were shocked at the prospect of fighting the mother country. These people, called *Loyalists*, were usually quieter than the rebels, but they could be found in large numbers in nearly every colony including South Carolina. People didn't necessarily fit neatly into one category, and many Americans were torn between these various ways of thinking.

King George III

The members of the Second Continental Congress, which opened in Philadelphia on May 10, 1775, were as scared and confused as everyone else. For a time South Carolina was represented at the Second Continental Congress by the same five men who attended the First Continental Congress. Soon after it opened, the Second Continental Congress sent a last-ditch attempt at making peace to King George III of England. Called the Olive Branch Petition, it stated

Congress's hope that "harmony between [Britain] and these Colonies may be restored." But peace was not restored.

On June 17, 1775, the Americans and the British fought the Battle of Bunker Hill, near Boston. Both sides suffered such heavy losses in this famous battle that their hatred for each other deepened. The Americans were also enraged when King George III not only rejected the Olive Branch Petition but also began hiring German soldiers, called *Hessians*, to fight on Britain's side. Events in South Carolina also proved that a major war was underway.

British and Hessian soldiers were sent to America to fight the patriots.

In portions of the Up Country, many of the people were Loyalists. One reason for this was that Up Country people felt more oppressed by the powerful Low Country lawmakers in Charleston than by the English government across the ocean. However, the patriots in and around Charleston were far stronger than the Up Country Loyalists .

The British tried to keep royal government alive for a time in South Carolina. In June 1775, Lord William Campbell arrived in Charleston as South Carolina's new royal governor. He turned out to be its *last* royal governor. For a short time South Carolina had two governments—the royal government with Lord William Campbell at its head, and the Provincial Congress, which was gaining strength. Governor Campbell's Up Country supporters were too far away from Charleston to help him. On September 15, 1775, a mob approached the house where Governor Campbell was staying. Campbell fled, taking refuge on a British ship in Charleston Harbor and ending royal government in South Carolina.

The rebels who controlled the governments in South Carolina and the other colonies were moving the country toward independence. In January 1776, New Hampshire became the first of the thirteen colonies to create a state government that was completely free of Great Britain. The Provincial Congress turned South Carolina into a state on March 26, 1776, when it adopted a state constitution (framework of government) and elected John Rutledge as the first state governor.

Meanwhile, fighting had broken out in South Carolina. From November 19 to 21, 1775, about 600 patriots exchanged gunfire with some 1,800 Loyalists at the town of Ninety Six in western South Carolina. One patriot and perhaps several Loyalists were killed in this skirmish, which was the first of more than 100 Revolutionary War battles fought in South Carolina. It was also the start of a tremendous amount of bloodshed between South Carolina's Loyalists and patriots.

One of the redcoats' goals was to capture Charleston. From Charleston, they could work their way north and conquer other colonies. In May 1776, South Carolinians learned that British ships were sailing toward Charleston. As part of the patriots' efforts to defend the South Carolina capital, Colonel William Moultrie was completing a fort on Sullivans Island at the entrance to Charleston Harbor. The island had many palmetto trees, so the patriots used palmetto logs to build the walls of this fortification, which became known as Fort Moultrie. While the fort was being

John Rutledge

Colonel William Moultrie

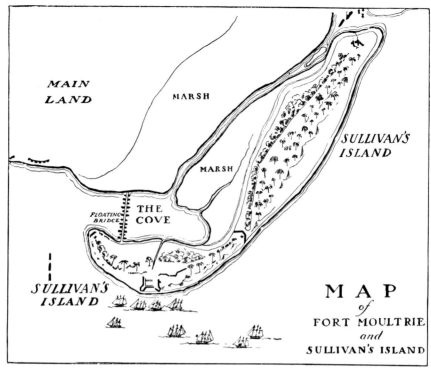

The palmetto-log Fort Moultrie on Sullivan's Island guarded the approach to Charleston by sea.

MAIN LAND

MARSH

MARSH

SULLIVAN'S ISLAND

FLOATING BRIDGE

THE COVE

SULLIVAN'S ISLAND

M A P
of
FORT MOULTRIE
and
SULLIVAN'S ISLAND

built, thousands of American soldiers, mostly South Carolinians, poured into Charleston to help defend the town.

Fort Moultrie was not finished when the British fleet approached in late June 1776. Colonel Moultrie raised a flag over the fort. It was all blue but for a silver crescent containing the word LIBERTY in one corner. Except that it had no palmetto tree, the flag resembled the South Carolina state flag of today. At ten o'clock on the morning of June 28, 1776, the British fleet attacked the fort.

The British thought the fort would soon fall under their ferocious fire, but they were in for a shock. The palmetto logs absorbed the cannon-balls much as a bulletin board absorbs thumbtacks. Colonel William Moultrie returned the cannon fire, damaging several British vessels and killing dozens of British troops. At one point, a British shell ripped down the South Carolina flag and Sergeant William Jasper performed a famous deed. He rushed out of the fort in the face of enemy fire and picked up the flag, which he tied to a stick and raised above the fort once more.

Sergeant William Jasper saving the flag at Fort Moultrie

At about 9:30 P.M., after pounding it with cannonballs for nearly twelve hours, the British gave up their attempt to take Fort Moultrie. More than 200 British troops had been killed or wounded in the battle, including about 100 on the warship *Bristol.* About 40 Americans had been killed or wounded. Unable to get past Fort Moultrie, the British gave up their efforts to seize Charleston—for the time being. Because the palmetto-log fort stood up so well and the men within it fought so bravely on that June day in 1776, the palmetto tree became South Carolina's best-known symbol. South Carolina was nick-named the Palmetto State, and pictures of palmetto trees were placed on its state flag and seal.

In Philadelphia, the Continental Congress was to vote on an extremely important matter a few days after the battle at Fort Moultrie. Should the colonies declare themselves independent of Great Britain? Each colony would vote yes or no on this issue, based on the majority opinion of its delegates. As the day of the vote neared, it appeared that most of the thirteen colonies would choose independence. But unless they *all* chose independence, the country could be divided, with some colonies forming a new nation and others remaining under British rule.

When Congress held a trial vote on July 1, 1776—the day before the official vote—nine colonies were found to favor independence. New York's delegates had been told not to vote on the issue. Two of Delaware's delegates were split, while the third was nearly 100 miles from Philadelphia in his home colony. Delegates from Pennsylvania and South Carolina were opposed. As Edward Rutledge, one of South Carolina's delegates, told Congress: "Right now I would call any declaration for independence a blind, precipitous measure!" In simpler words, he felt that America wasn't ready for independence. South Carolinians were also afraid that if they became part of a new country, it would be dominated by the Northern states, which might try to end slavery. Yet Rutledge also told Congress that South Carolina might change its position when the official vote was made the next day.

Edward Rutledge.

Late on the afternoon of July 2, 1776, the vote was counted. The nine states that had favored independence the day before held firm. Pennsylvania squeaked by in favor of independence—only because two delegates who were opposed decided not to vote. Caesar Rodney made an all-night and all-day ride through stormy weather to swing

Caesar Rodney

Thomas Jefferson

Delaware's vote in favor of independence. And South Carolina did change its vote as Edward Rutledge had hinted. Edward Rutledge explained that South Carolina didn't want to be the only colony voting against independence. Although New York's delegates didn't vote on July 2, they made the independence vote unanimous a few days later.

On July 4, 1776, Congress approved the Declaration of Independence, which Virginia's Thomas Jefferson had written to explain why the thirteen colonies were becoming the United States of America. Ever since, the Fourth of July has been celebrated as the United States' birthday. By the time most members of the Continental Congress signed the Declaration of Independence in the summer of 1776, Christopher Gadsden and John Rutledge had left Congress; Thomas Lynch had become very ill and had been replaced by his son, Thomas Lynch, Jr.; Henry Middleton had been replaced by his son, Arthur Middleton; and Thomas Heyward, Jr., had been added as a South Carolina delegate. Edward Rutledge, Thomas Heyward, Jr., Thomas Lynch, Jr., and Arthur Middleton signed the Declaration for the Palmetto State. At just twenty-six years of age, Edward Rutledge was the youngest signer of the Declara-

Left to right: Thomas Lynch, Jr., Arthur Middleton, Thomas Heyward, Jr.

tion. When the Declaration was read aloud in Charleston in early August, people cheered, cannons were fired, and there was a parade of lawmakers and army officers through the South Carolina capital.

Important though it was, the Declaration of Independence was still just a piece of paper. Independence had to be won with bullets and cannonballs. England's army and navy were so much stronger than America's that for several years it looked as though the United States was about to be squashed back into the thirteen colonies, like Cinderella's coach turned back into a pumpkin at the stroke of midnight. Much of the credit for keeping the American cause alive must go to George Washington, the American commander, who kept most of the American losses small by avoiding big battles during the war's early years.

From the time of the failed British attempt to seize Charleston in 1776 until 1780, all the major Revolutionary War battles were fought in the Northern states. One big threat to South Carolina came from the Cherokee, who took Britain's side because they hated the American patriots for taking their lands. Just a few days after the British assault on Charleston in 1776, the Cherokee began attacking families and burning cabins along the South Carolina frontier. A 4,000-man army composed mostly of South Carolinians but also including some Virginians and North Carolinians sought revenge on the Cherokee. The American forces killed perhaps 2,000 Cherokee along the frontier and destroyed many of their towns. In 1777 the defeated Cherokee turned over a huge tract of land that became South Carolina's four far western counties.

Just as the Cherokee saw the Revolutionary War as a chance to strike back at the Americans, France saw it as an opportunity to hurt England, its old enemy. In the spring of 1778, France entered the war on America's side. This gradually turned the tide in favor of the Americans, but not until the patriots endured more hard times.

Although the British had seized New York City and Philadelphia, they had not completely conquered the North as they had hoped. In 1778 Britain shifted its main focus from the Northern to the Southern states. British leaders knew that the Carolinas and Georgia had large numbers of people who kept their loyalty to the mother country quiet out of fear that the patriots who controlled the state governments would punish them. The British figured that if they could conquer such key Southern towns as Charleston, South Carolina, and Savannah, Georgia, thousands of these Loyalists would come out of the woodwork. These people could help the redcoats conquer the entire South and then later the North.

The British poured thousands of men into Savannah in late 1778 and seized the town that

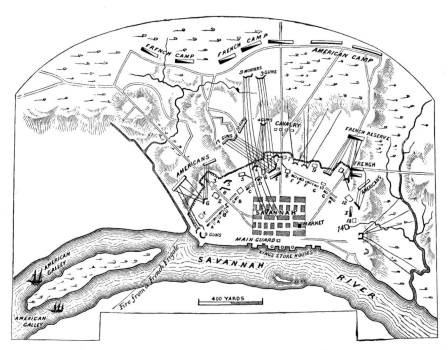

Plan of the siege of Savannah

British troops at the siege of Charleston.

December. Then in February 1780, a British fleet carrying more than 10,000 men approached Charleston from the sea. The Americans tried to defend Charleston for a time, but the cause was hopeless. Although Governor John Rutledge and most of the state lawmakers escaped Charleston, more than 5,000 American troops were captured when the British seized the town on May 12, 1780. The entire American army was never larger than 20,000 men at any time during the war, so the loss of 5,000 men at Charleston was a horrible blow. The British quickly seized much of the rest of South Carolina, establishing military posts at such towns as Ninety Six, Camden, and Georgetown. The British also invaded North Carolina in 1780.

As the British had hoped, their takeover of parts of Georgia and the Carolinas brought thousands of Loyalists out of the woodwork. In 1780-81 there were many bloody fights between bands of Loyalists and patriots in South Carolina. The Loyalists had the upper hand, and they brutally murdered so many patriots that even the redcoats were shocked.

The patriot cause was kept alive in South Carolina largely through guerrilla warfare—the Native American style of fighting with raids and ambushes. Three famous South Carolinians led the guerrilla warfare against the British and the Loyalists. Francis Marion, known as the Swamp Fox, led raids on the enemy in the Low Country. Thomas Sumter, the Gamecock (a gamecock is a fighting rooster), led raids in the middle of the state. Andrew Pickens led raids in western South Carolina. In 1780-81 the Palmetto State was also the scene of three major battles at Camden, Kings Mountain, and Cowpens.

The redcoats seized Camden, a town near the middle of South Carolina, a few days after taking

Horatio Gates

Charleston in the spring of 1780. Camden became the main British headquarters in central South Carolina. It was said that the British executed so many American patriots in Camden that its streets ran red with blood for a year. General Horatio Gates, commander of the American forces in the South, wanted to capture Camden from the British. In August 1780, Gates approached Camden with 3,000 men—seemingly enough to overcome the several hundred redcoats in the town. However, British general Charles Cornwallis learned of Gates's plan and headed toward him with about 2,000 men. Gates's and Cornwallis's troops clashed five miles outside Camden before dawn on August 16, 1780. The Battle of Camden was a total British victory. Not only were 1,000 Americans killed or wounded, compared with about 300 British, but Gates and many of his men fled the battlefield in terror.

After their victory at Camden, the British felt certain that the Americans were no match for them. Major Patrick Ferguson, a Scottish-born soldier on the British side, boasted that the mother country's forces would "hang their [the Americans'] leaders, and lay their country waste with fire and sword." Ferguson led more than 1,000 Loyalist troops from the Carolinas and several other states, so he seemed capable of backing up his words.

About 1,000 frontiersmen from North and South Carolina, Virginia, Georgia, and Tennessee decided to attack Ferguson and his Loyalists. Under their leader, Colonel William Campbell, the backwoods patriots tracked Ferguson to a ridge of Kings Mountain, in the far northern part of the Palmetto State near the North Carolina border. Reportedly, Ferguson was so sure that his position was safe that he said something like "God Almighty could not drive us from the mountain!"

On the afternoon of October 7, 1780, the Americans crept up toward Ferguson and his men. The two sides fought a tremendous battle on Kings Mountain. After Major Ferguson and many of his men were killed, the Loyalists raised the

The death of Major Patrick Ferguson at Kings Mountain

white flag of surrender, but the Americans were so thirsty for enemy blood that they ignored the rules of warfare and fought a few minutes more. By the time the hour-long battle ended, all of Ferguson's men had been killed, wounded, or captured, compared with about 100 Americans. The defeat at Kings Mountain was a terrible blow to the English.

The month that the Americans won the Battle of Kings Mountain, George Washington named General Nathanael Greene to replace Gates as the commander of the Southern army. Greene was a better leader than Gates. One of Greene's best decisions was to send out General Daniel Morgan with 1,000 men to face the British. At a place called Cowpens (because cattle were penned there) in far northern South Carolina, Morgan and his

Left to right: Nathanael Greene, Daniel Morgan, Banastre Tarleton

Revolutionary War battles in the South

men demolished a slightly larger English force under Colonel Banastre Tarleton on January 17, 1781. Nearly all of Tarleton's 1,100 troops were killed, wounded, or captured at the Battle of Cowpens.

Because of their losses at Kings Mountain, Cowpens, and other places in the Carolinas, a

General Cornwallis surrenders the British army to the American forces at Yorktown.

Article 14th
No Article of the Capitula
tion to be infringed on pre-
text of Reprisal, & if there be
any doubtfull Expressions
in it, they are to be interpreted according to the common meaning & acceptation
of the Words. —

Done at York in Virginia
this 19th day of October 1781

Cornwallis
Tho: Symonds

The capitulation of Yorktown

huge British force of 8,000 men withdrew to Yorktown, Virginia, in the summer of 1781. That fall, the British troops at Yorktown were surrounded by George Washington's 17,000-man army on land and by French ships at sea. Washington's forces pounded the British position day after day. With no place to hide, 7,200 British troops surrendered to General Washington on October 19, 1781. The great American victory at Yorktown meant that the United States had won the Revolutionary War. In 1783 Great Britain signed a peace treaty acknowledging that the thirteen colonies had become a new nation: the United States of America.

HENRY LAURENS (1724-1792)

Henry Laurens was born in Charleston into a well-to-do family of French Huguenots. As a child, he made friends with another Charleston boy, Christopher Gadsden, who was just a few days older than he. Henry Laurens was trained for business by his father, a Charleston merchant. At the age of twenty Henry was sent to England, where he worked for a large merchant firm for about three years. Upon his return to Charleston in June 1747, his happiness at being home was instantly shattered. He learned that his father hadn't met him at the dock because he had died four days earlier.

Henry went into business in Charleston and within a few years was one of South Carolina's leading merchants. His reputation as a skillful, honest businessman was so high that just having worked for him was viewed as a recommendation. For the most part, Henry handled business deals for others, selling such goods as rice, indigo, and deerskins, and buying slaves and wine for a commission. He invested much of his money in land, and eventually owned about 20,000 acres (about 30 square miles) in South Carolina and Georgia.

In 1757 Henry Laurens was elected to the South Carolina Commons House of Assembly, where he served almost continually until the Revolutionary War. He was an honest and brave lawmaker at a time when standards for politicians were very low. Everyone knew that if Henry Laurens felt he was right about an issue, no power on earth could shake him.

At the start of the troubles with England, Laurens felt that some people, including Christopher Gadsden, were too warlike. Many of the patriots, on the other hand, felt that Laurens was too willing to make up with England, and some even considered him a Loyalist. During the Stamp Act crisis in 1765, a mob came to his house in Charleston. "Open your doors and let us search your house and cellars!" the men demanded, suspecting that Laurens had hidden some of the stamps in his home. Laurens pointed out that he, too, hated the Stamp Act, but that he wouldn't let a mob search his home. He also offered to take out his pistols and duel any one of them man to man. The men apologized and left his house.

Once the war actually began, Laurens wholeheartedly took the patriots' side. He served as president of South Carolina's Provincial Congress and in 1776 helped write its first state constitution. Early the next year he was elected to the Continental Congress, where he served as its president for about a year. While in Congress, he was known to work eighteen or even twenty hours a day.

In 1780 Congress sent Laurens off to The Netherlands to obtain money that the new country desperately needed. On the way, Laurens's ship was

Henry Laurens

captured by the British. Henry Laurens was shipped off to England, where he was locked in the Tower of London. During his fifteen months in this prison, Laurens was poorly fed and neglected, and as a result he became very ill. When he was finally placed on trial, Laurens could no longer stand and had to be carried into the courtroom on a chair. He was accused of being an enemy to England. "I hold myself to be a citizen of the united, free, and independent states of North America, and will not do any act which shall involve me in an acknowledgment of subjection to this realm," Laurens said at his trial. By this time the Americans had won the Battle of Yorktown, and the British decided to let Laurens go.

Soon after his release, Henry Laurens was appointed by Congress to help make the peace treaty ending the Revolutionary War. He helped negotiate the treaty in Paris, France, then finally returned to America in 1784. Some people wanted to make him president of the Continental Congress once more, but his health had been wrecked by his treatment in prison. He lived his last seven years at his plantation—Mepkin—about thirty miles outside Charleston, where he died at the age of sixty-eight. Laurens County in western South Carolina was named for Henry Laurens.

JOHN LAURENS (1754–1782)

John Laurens

When Henry Laurens was twenty-six years old, he married Eleanor Ball, a nineteen-year-old South Carolinian. The couple had at least twelve children, only four of whom lived to adulthood. Henry was especially close to his son, John, who was born in Charleston the year that the French and Indian War began. John was taught by tutors in Charleston, and then in 1771, not long after his mother died, he was sent to study in Switzerland and England.

John was studying law in England when the Revolutionary War began. Many people in his shoes would have continued their studies and avoided involvement in the war. Not only had John been away from America for several years, he had also married an English girl. Nonetheless, John said good-bye to his wife and newborn baby in early 1777 and returned to Charleston to fight for his country.

Soon after reaching home, John Laurens joined George Washington's "family," as the American commander called his staff. John went on a number of secret missions for Washington, and also fought in a number of battles. His first action was at the Battle of Brandywine, fought in

Pennsylvania on September 11, 1777. In a letter to his father, John provided a vivid description of this battle, in which he was shot in the ankle:

> There was a most infernal fire of cannon and musketry; smoke; incessant shouting, "Incline to the right!" "Incline to the left!" "Halt!" "Charge!" The balls [were] ploughing up the ground; the trees cracking over one's head; the branches riven by the artillery; the leaves falling as in autumn, by the grape shot. . . . A ball glanced about my ankle and [injured] it; for some days I was lifted off and on horseback in men's arms. . . .

Despite his wound, John fought at the Battle of Germantown, also in Pennsylvania, twenty-three days later. At this battle John and a few other men tried to burn down a house containing about 120 redcoats, but the enemy opened fire, seriously wounding John in the shoulder. Acts like this led George Washington to say that John had just one fault—he was so brave that he was sometimes reckless.

John was involved in a strange incident after the Battle of Monmouth, which was fought in New Jersey in June 1778. General Charles Lee, an English-born soldier fighting on the American side, behaved strangely at this battle. By waiting too long to attack and then telling his men to retreat without cause, Lee helped prevent this battle from being an American victory. Later it was learned that Lee probably had tried to lose the Battle of Monmouth because he had secretly joined the British side, but at the time Lee blamed George Washington for a poor battle plan. John Laurens was so angry over this insult to Washington that he challenged Charles Lee to a pistol duel. Laurens was wounded slightly and Lee was wounded severely in their duel, which was a rare example of a man fighting over a friend's honor rather than his own. Lee was later dismissed from the army because of his actions at the Battle of Monmouth.

John Laurens lived less than four years after his duel with Lee in late 1778, but those years were packed with action. He fought to defend Charleston in 1780, and was one of the more than 5,000 men seized when the redcoats captured the South Carolina capital. He was freed in a prisoner exchange after several months. The Continental Congress then sent John to France to obtain aid for America. John succeeded, but as was often the case with him, he did it in his own unusual way. He was expected to work through the king's assistants, but since they weren't very helpful, he went straight to King Louis XVI and handed him his request. The result was that France soon sent a fleet of ships loaded with money and military supplies to America. This aid helped the United States win the war a short time later.

John returned to America just in time to fight in the last big battle of the war at Yorktown, Virginia, where he took eighty men and stormed a British outpost, capturing its commanding officer. John was also given the job of arranging the surrender terms with the redcoats after the battle.

Following the Battle of Yorktown, there were some minor skirmishes before the peace treaty was made in 1783. In one of them, fought along South Carolina's Combahee River on August 27, 1782, twenty-seven-year-old John Laurens was shot and killed while leading a band of men against a British force three times as large.

One reason John Laurens isn't very well known today is that he died young, and another is that he held an unpopular view for his time. John thought it was outrageous for people to speak of "liberty" while enslaving thousands of black people. He wanted to end slavery, and created a plan by which South Carolina slaves could earn their freedom by fighting against England. The idea of arming and freeing slaves scared and angered white South Carolinians, and so the state legislature voted down John's plan. It took more than a century for most white Southerners to catch up to John Lauren's way of thinking about slavery.

CHRISTOPHER GADSDEN (1724–1805)

Christopher Gadsden

Christopher Gadsden was born in Charleston just a few days before his boyhood friend, Henry Laurens. Christopher's mother died when he was just three years old. The boy obtained his love of learning from his father, who owned about 125 books, a large library for the time. He also grew to dislike gambling because of his father, who once lost sixty-three acres of land near Charleston in a card game.

At about the age of eight, Christopher was sent to England, where he lived and attended school for about eight years. He returned to America at sixteen to take a job his father had arranged for him with a merchant in Philadelphia. A short time later, Mr. Gadsden died, leaving seventeen-year-old Christopher a fortune, but also leaving him an orphan and on his own in Philadelphia.

When he turned twenty-one, Christopher left his job with the Philadelphia merchant. Before entering business for himself in Charleston, he sailed to England to visit relatives. While returning to America on the warship *Aldborough*, Christopher was asked by the captain to become the ship's *purser* (bookkeeper). King George's War (1744–1748) against France had begun, and Christopher wanted to help the mother country any way he could. He delayed his business career and for the next three years sailed to such places as Canada, Boston, New York City, Jamaica, and Barbados. When the war ended in 1748, he returned to Charleston.

Christopher Gadsden was soon one of Charleston's most prominent men. In 1757 he was elected to the South Carolina legislature, where he served for nearly thirty years. By 1761 he owned several stores and a great deal of land. One thing he did with his money was buy back much of the land that his father had gambled away in the card game.

When the troubles with England began, Christopher turned against England earlier and more fiercely than just about anyone else in South Carolina. In 1765 he represented South Carolina at the Stamp Act Congress in New York City, where he and James Otis of Massachusetts were the strongest opponents of the British Parliament. Gadsden also wrote many newspaper articles attacking the Stamp Act and was a leader of Charleston's Sons of Liberty.

Judging by his writings, Gadsden seems to have favored American independence by about 1769—earlier than nearly every other well-known colonist. Gadsden represented South Carolina at both Continental Congresses. At the First Continental Congress he gave a fiery speech in which he said, "Our seaport towns are composed of brick and wood. If they are destroyed we have clay and lumber enough to rebuild them. But if the liberties of our country are destroyed, where shall we find the materials to replace them?" It is thought that at the Second Continental Congress Gadsden helped found the Continental Navy (forerunner of the U.S. Navy) and designed its famous early flag, which featured a picture of a coiled rattlesnake along with the warning DON'T TREAD ON ME.

Some people wondered if Christopher would be willing to fight for the liberty about which he so often spoke. When the British attacked Charleston in the spring of 1780, most of the lawmakers fled the town to avoid capture. Gadsden, who was South Carolina's lieutenant governor, refused to leave. When the redcoats closed in, Gadsden said that he would die before he surrendered. Fortunately, though, he soon realized that there was no choice but to surrender.

The British sent Christopher Gadsden to a fort in Florida, which was then under their rule, where he spent ten months in a dungeon. He was allowed no visitors, and the British soldiers who brought him food wouldn't tell him what was occurring in the war. The "Flame of Liberty," as Gadsden was called, spent much of his time reading his Hebrew books by candlelight. He was finally released in the summer of 1781, several months before the British surrender at Yorktown. Early the next year Gadsden was elected governor of South Carolina, but he refused the office because the months in prison had destroyed his health, much as had happened to his boyhood friend Henry Laurens. Although Gadsden now suffered dizzy spells and periods when his memory failed, he lived many more years. The "Flame of Liberty" died in his beloved Charleston at the age of eighty-one.

FRANCIS MARION (1732–1795)

Francis Marion

Francis Marion was born on a farm in South Carolina's Berkeley County, not far from Charleston. Like Henry and John Laurens, he was of French Huguenot ancestry. Francis was scrawny and sickly as a child, so at about the age of fifteen he decided to become a sailor to build himself up and escape farm work. Francis signed up for a voyage to the West Indies that ended in an unusual disaster when a whale smashed into the vessel. The sailors managed to escape in a lifeboat before their ship sank, but after they had been adrift for about a week, two of them died, probably of hunger and thirst. Francis and the others survived until they reached land by eating a pet dog they had rescued from the sinking ship. This experience toughened Francis, but dry land looked great to him from then on, and he never went to sea again!

When Francis was in his twenties, he joined the colonial army that fought the Cherokee during the French and Indian War. In a battle in June 1761, Francis was ordered to take thirty men and attack the Cherokee before the main colonial force entered the fight. Francis was remarkably cool under fire, even though twenty-one of his thirty men were killed or wounded. He helped the colonists win this battle, and soon the Cherokee were crushed, and many of their towns lay in ashes. One of Marion's finest qualities was his feeling for his defeated enemies. Regarding the destruction of the Cherokee settlements, he reportedly said, "To me it appeared a shocking sight. When we are gone the Indian children will return and ask their mothers, 'Who did this?' 'The white people, the Christians,' will be the reply."

Francis lived peacefully as a farmer for about fifteen years after the victory over the Cherokee. When the war with Britain began, South Carolinians turned to Marion. He was elected to South Carolina's Provincial Congress of 1775, and that June the Provincial Congress elected him as a captain of the troops that the colony was raising.

Francis Marion served in campaigns in and near Charleston for about the next four years. He helped defend the palmetto-log Fort Moultrie from the British fleet in June 1776. In the spring of 1780, he was helping to prepare Charleston for another British assault when he had a very lucky "break." An American officer who lived in Charleston invited Marion and some other soldiers to a dinner party. The host locked the door, saying that they must all get drunk. Marion hated drunkenness, so he jumped from a second-floor window to escape, breaking his ankle. No longer able to help defend Charleston, Francis went to friends and relatives in his home region along South Carolina's Santee River. What made this injury a lucky "break" was the fact that he wasn't among the American troops who were captured when the British seized Charleston several weeks later.

The redcoats were soon in control of most of South Carolina. In 1780, Francis organized "Marion's Brigade," the most famous of the guerrilla bands that continued the fight for liberty. Usually numbering around a hundred, Marion's troops slept in swamps and forests where the British couldn't find them. Then in the dead of night they would emerge from their hiding places and strike. They destroyed enemy supplies, released American prisoners, captured British troops, and kept patriot leaders informed of the redcoats' movements. But their greatest contribution lay in keeping the patriots' hopes alive in South Carolina until the American army won battles in the South near the end of the war.

The redcoats wanted to capture Marion, but he was so elusive that one British officer said, "As for this damned swamp fox, the Devil himself could not catch him!" The nickname Swamp Fox stuck. Thanks to a man who fought under him, we know what the Swamp Fox looked like at the height of his activities. He was barely over five feet tall and limped on the ankle that had been broken. He had steady, black, piercing eyes, and on his head he wore a leather cap with a silver crescent and the words "LIBERTY OR DEATH" on it.

The greatest battle in which Marion's Brigade fought was the Battle of Eutaw Springs, which took place on September 8, 1781, in the area now covered by South Carolina's Lake Marion. Thanks partly to the Swamp Fox and his men, nearly half the British troops were killed or wounded in this battle. A few weeks later, the fighting ended with the Battle of Yorktown.

Francis Marion served as a South Carolina state lawmaker after the war. Unlike many people who sought revenge against the Loyalists, Marion preached forgiveness. "God has given us the victory," he said. "Let us show our gratitude to heaven, which we shall not do by cruelty to man." The Swamp Fox married for the first and only time in the spring of 1786 at the age of fifty-four. Just before he died at his South Carolina plantation at the age of sixty-three, he told his wife, "I am not afraid to die, for thank God, I can lay my hand upon my heart and say that since I came to man's estate, I have never intentionally done wrong to any man." South Carolina's Marion County and the city of Marion were named for the Swamp Fox, as was the artificial Lake Marion.

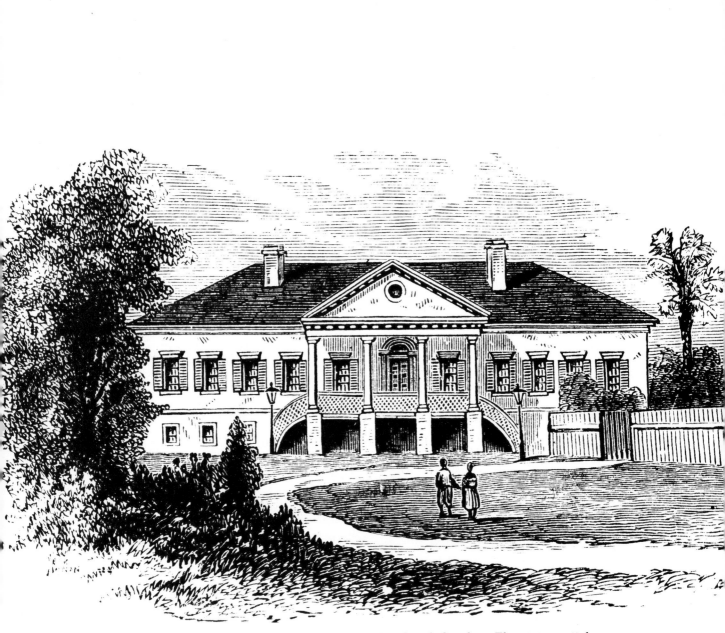

The Old State House at Columbia, South Carolina. The state capital was moved from Charleston to Columbia in 1790.

Chapter VIII

The Eighth State!

Our government must be suitable to the people, and we are perhaps the only people in the world who ever had sense enough to appoint delegates to establish a general government.

Charles Pinckney, speaking at the Constitutional Convention in 1787

Against all odds, America had beaten the world's strongest nation to win its freedom. But once the war ended, it appeared that if England or another country waited just a few years, the United States would topple with just a little shove. Although each state was rather strong, the United States as a nation was weak. In fact, there really was no unified nation as we think of it today. Instead, the thirteen states were more like thirteen separate countries.

The nation was governed by the Articles of Confederation, which took effect in the spring of 1781. Under these laws, the country had a weak central government still called the Continental Congress. Two "Henrys" from South Carolina were among the presidents of the Continental Congress—Henry Middleton, who served from October 22, 1774, to May 10, 1775, and Henry Laurens, who served from November 1, 1777, to December 9, 1778. The president of the Continental Congress had a tiny fraction of the power that the president of the United States was later given.

Besides having no strong president to lead it, the United States had many other problems. There were no national courts, which meant that cases affecting the whole country were difficult to settle. There were no national taxes, which meant that the government could not pay all its bills. And there was just a tiny U.S. army, which meant that the country could not defend itself properly. Often many Americans didn't even know where their national capital was located, because there was no permanent capital. Instead, the government moved from town to town like an orphan.

The central government was weak because most Americans wanted it that way. Nearly everyone was afraid that a strong government would do what the English had tried—tax them! The Americans had made it clear what they thought about that. There was also plenty of hostility between the states. Southerners feared that

Shays' mob takes possession of a courthouse

Northerners would seize control of a strong central government, and then outlaw slavery. Small states feared that large states would run the central government.

However, several events of the 1780s proved to most people that the central government had to be strengthened. One was Shays' Rebellion, a

John Rutledge

Charles Pinckney

Charles Cotesworth
Pinckney

Pierce Butler

revolt by western Massachusetts farmers that took place from September 1786 to February 1787. The 700-man U.S. Army couldn't end this revolt, so the Massachusetts militia did the job. If the country's army couldn't handle a revolt by farmers in one part of one state, what would happen if there was a major threat to the nation?

Between May and September 1787, American leaders met at Philadelphia, Pennsylvania, to create a stronger central government. Rhode Island was the only state that failed to send delegates to this convention. South Carolina's delegates were John Rutledge, Charles Pinckney and his cousin Charles Cotesworth Pinckney, and Pierce Butler.

At first the delegates planned just to strengthen the Articles of Confederation, but instead they threw the Articles into the wastebasket and produced a new framework of government, the United States Constitution. The Constitution created a far stronger national government than had existed under the Articles.

Everything didn't go smoothly at the Constitutional Convention. Some Northern delegates hoped to outlaw slavery, but if they had, the South Carolina and Georgia delegates would have walked out of the convention. Slavery was allowed to continue, and as a result the Civil War was fought partly over this issue less than a century later. South Carolina's four delegates signed the Constitution for the Palmetto State.

Each state was to join the country under the new Constitution when it approved the paper. Once nine states had approved, the Constitution would take effect. Delaware earned its nickname, the First State, by approving the Constitution on December 7, 1787—before any of the other twelve states. Several states followed, and then on April 28, 1788, Maryland became the seventh state, meaning that just two more states had to approve the Constitution to make it the law of the land.

In May 1788, South Carolina leaders met in Charleston to vote on whether to approve or reject the Constitution. Had this convention represented the people fairly, it probably would have voted down the Constitution, because the Up Country people who made up the bulk of South Carolina's white population generally opposed the Constitution. They ran smaller farms and wanted to be left alone by the government and the rest of the world. The Low Country people, who comprised far less than half of South Carolina's white population, generally felt that a stronger federal government would protect their wealth, and so

The signers of the U.S. Constitution

they favored the Constitution. As was true in the state government, though, Low Country people were allowed an unfairly large number of delegates at the South Carolina convention that voted on the Constitution. The delegates approved the Constitution by a 149 to 73 vote on May 23, 1788, transforming South Carolina into the eighth state. This vote set the stage for the Constitution to become the law of the land a month later when New Hampshire became the ninth state to approve it.

Over the next few years, the Up Country demanded and won more representation in the South Carolina state legislature. Something else happened in the late 1700s that made Up Country people happy. Charleston had served well as South Carolina's capital for 120 years, from the founding of South Carolina to the early years of statehood. Now it was time for the people in the interior of the state to have the capital closer to them. In 1790 the capital of the Palmetto State was moved from Charleston to Columbia, a new town in almost the exact center of the state, where it has been ever since.

The State House at Columbia in 1794. Inset:
The Seal of the state of South Carolina.

THE
Fundamental Conftitutions
OF
C A R O L I N A

OUR Sovereign Lord the King having out of His Royal Grace and Bounty, granted unto us the Province of *Caro-lina*, with all the Royalties, Proprieties, Jurifdictions and Privileges of a *County Palatine*, as large and ample as the County Palatine of *Durham*, with other great Privileges; for the better Settlement of the Government of the faid Place, and, efta-blifhing the Intereft of the Lords Proprietors with Equality, and without Confufion, and that the Government of this Province may be made moft agreeable to the Monarchy under which we live, and of which this Province is a Part; and that we may avoid erecting a numerous *Democracy*, we the *Lords* and *Proprietors* of the Province aforefaid, have agreed to this following Form of *Government*, to be perpetually eftablifhed amongft us, unto which we do oblige ourfelves, our Heirs and Succeffors, in the moft binding Ways that can be devifed.

§. 1. THE *Eldeft* of the *Lords Proprietors* fhall be *Palatine*, and upon the Deceafe of the *Palatine*, the *Eldeft* of the Seven furviving *Proprietors* fhall always fucceed him.

§. 2. There fhall be *Seven* other *Chief Offices* erected, *viz.* The *Admirals*, *Chamberlains*, *Chancellors*, *Conftables*, *Chief-Juftices*, *High-Stewards* and *Treafurers*; which Places fhall be enjoy'd by none but the *Lords Proprietors*, to be affign'd at firft by Lot, and upon the Vacancy of any one of the Seven Great Offices by Death, or other-wife, the Eldeft *Proprietor* fhall have his Choice of the faid Place.

§. 3. The whole Province fhall be *divided into Counties*, each Coun-ty fhall confift of Eight *Signiories*, Eight *Baronies*, and Four *Precincts*; each *Precinct* fhall confift of Six *Colonies*.

F   §. 4. Each

The Fundamental Constitutions was a frame of government made for the Carolina colony by the Lords Proprietors.

THE
South-Carolina Gazette.

NUMB. 77.

Containing the freſheſt Advices Foreign and Domeſtick.

From 𝔖aturðap, JULY 12. to 𝔖aturðap, JULY 19. 1735.

CHARLES-TOWN, July 19.

ON Sunday laſt arrived here Capt. *Hugh Percy* in 9 Weeks from *Rotterdam* and 6 from *Cowes*, with 250 *Switzers* on board, who are come to ſettle a Townſhip on the King's Land in this Province upon the Encouragement granted to other Foreigners. Amongſt them are Ninety fit to bear Arms, and it is not doubted but their ſettling in this Province will much contribute to its Strength, and by their Induſtry and Laborioufneſs tend to its great Advantage; there being in ſome parts of this Province very good Land for Wheat and Corn, they may probably upon proper Encouragement furniſh us in time with a good Quantity of that neceſſary and ſo much wanting Commodity, which now we are obliged to purchaſe at what rate ſoever from our neighbours.

The Province of *Penſſylvania*, to which theſe ſeveral Years paſt many thouſands (ſome will ſay above 70,000) of perſecuted Palatines and Switzers have taken their refuge, is thereby brought in ſuch a flouriſhing Condition, that between the 25th of March 1734, and the 25th of March 1735 from thence is exported Wheat, 195,05 Buſhels, 1300 Tierces, *Indian Corn*, 10464 Buſhels, *Flour* 37,231 Barrels, 1536 Half-barrels; *Bread* 3232 Tierces, 8474 Barrels, 693 Half-barrels and 681 Qu. Casks.

On Thurſday His Honour the Lieutenant Governor being petitioned by thoſe Switzers, that they might be qualified, in order to enjoy the ſame Privileges and Liberties as natural born Subjects of the King of *England*, called a Council, and directed *Tho: Dale, Tho: Lamboll* and *Henry Gibbes* Eſqrs; three of his Majeſty's Juſtices of the Peace, to adminiſter to ſo many of them as deſired it the Oath of Allegiance and to let them ſubſcribe the Teſt, according to a Law made for that purpoſe, when accordingly in the Afternoon the ſame were read to Seventy-ſix of them then preſent, (ſome being ſick and abſent to the Number of

Fourteen) in the *German* Tongue by an Interpreter ſworn to that purpoſe, and having explain'd to them the meaning of it, and they all being willing to take this Oath, the ſame was again read in Engliſh by one of the aforeſaid his Majeſty's Juſtices, and interpreted by ſhort Sentences, which they all repeated, and at the Concluſion ſubſcribed to the aforeſaid Oath and Teſt.

They are to ſettle a Townſhip upon *Ediſto* River, which is thought the beſt Ground for Wheat, Corn, Hemp and Flax, as alſo for planting of Vineyards.

The Ship *St. Andrew*, Capt. *Peter Robinſon*, came out the ſame Time with Capt. *Percy* from *Cowes*, having on board about 200 Palatines, and is expected here every Day.

Laſt Week were preſented to the Grand Jury at *Savannah*, Bills of Indictment againſt *Thomas Mellichamp* and *Richard Turner*, for Counterfeiting current Money Bills of this Province, and iſſuing the ſame knowing them to be Counterfeits: That againſt *Mellichamp* was returned *Ignoramus*, the other *Billa vera*, the Evidence being full it's thought he will be found Guilty by the Petty Jury, as a Cheat; upon the Evidence it appeared, That *Turner* was directed by old Mr. *Mellichamp* to make ſuch a Preſs as he had in his Iſland, that *Turner* did make ſuch another, that he was privy to all the Steps taken by him in ſtamping the ſaid Bills: His two Servants were Evidences againſt him, who were Witneſſes to the ſeveral Actions of *Mellichamp* and their Matter.

Capt. *Percy* informs us, That Admiral *Norris* with a Squadron of 27 Men of War, is gone to aſſiſt the King of *Portugal* againſt the King of *Spain*, they having confined each other's Ambaſſadors, as well as impriſoned their Domeſticks: This Rupture is occaſioned, as 'tis ſaid, by the King of *Portugal* ſupplying the Emperor with Money. We have by the ſaid Captain ſome publick Prints, out of which we have taken the following Articles of

FO-

The *South-Carolina Gazette* began publishing in 1732 and lasted for over fifty years.

Ad for a quartet of Africans who declined the hospitality of their new "owner" and voted with their feet. Anxieties about controlling slaves led to a series of eighteenth-century laws called slave codes. The excerpt shown here is from an act "better ordering and controlling negroes and other slaves."

---

398   STATUTES AT LARGE

A.D. 1740.   *Acts relating to Slaves.*

person or persons whatsoever, on his or her behalf, to apply to the justices of his Majesty's court of common pleas, by petition or motion, either during the sitting of the said court, or before any of the justices of the same court, at any time in the vacation; and the said court, or any of the justices thereof, shall, and they are hereby fully impowered to, admit any person so applying to be guardian for any negro, Indian, mulatto or mustizo, claiming his, her or their freedom; and such guardians shall be enabled, entitled and capable in law, to bring an action of trespass in the nature of ravishment of ward, against any person who shall claim property in, or who shall be in possession of, any such negro, Indian, mulatto or mustizo; and the defendant shall and may plead the general issue on such action brought, and the special matter may and shall be given in evidence, and upon a general or special verdict found, judgment shall be given according to the very right of the cause, without having any regard to any defect in the proceedings, either in form or substance; and if judgment shall be given for the plaintiff, a special entry shall be made, declaring that the ward of the plaintiff is free, and the jury shall assess damages which the plaintiff's ward hath sustained, and the court shall give judgment, and award execution, against the defendant for such damage, with full costs of suit; but in case judgment shall be given for the defendant, the said court is hereby fully impowered to inflict such corporal punishment, not extending to life or limb, on the ward of the plaintiff, as they, in their discretion, shall think fit; *provided always*, that in any action or suit to be brought in pursuance of the direction of this Act, the burthen of the proof shall lay on the plaintiff, and it shall be always presumed that every negro, Indian, mulatto and mustizo, is a slave, unless the contrary can be made appear, the Indians in amity with this government excepted, in which case the burthen of the proof shall lye on the defendant; *provided also*, that nothing in this Act shall be construed to hinder or restrain any other court of law or equity in this Province, from determining the property of slaves, or their right of freedom, which now have cognizance or jurisdiction of the same, when the same shall happen to come in judgment before such courts, or any of them, always taking this Act for their direction therein.

II. *And be it further enacted* by the authority aforesaid, That in every Recognizance. action or suit to be brought by any such guardian as aforesaid, appointed pursuant to the direction of this Act, the defendant shall enter into a recognizance, with one or more sufficient sureties, to the plaintiff, in such sum as the said court of common pleas shall direct, with condition that he shall produce the ward of the plaintiff at all times when required by the said court, and that whilst such action or suit shall be depending and undetermined, the ward of the plaintiff shall not be eloined, abused or misused.

III. And for the better keeping slaves in due order and subjection, *Be it* No slave to be *further enacted* by the authority aforesaid, That no person whatsoever shall absent from permit or suffer any slave under his or their care or management, and who home without lives or is employed in Charlestown, or any other town in this Province, a ticket. to go out of the limits of the said town, or any such slave who lives in the country, to go out of the plantation to which such slave belongs, or in which plantation such slave is usually employed, without a letter superscribed and directed, or a ticket in the words following:

Permit this slave to be absent from Charlestown, (or any other town, or if he lives in the country, from Mr. ——— plantation, ——— parish,) for ——— days or hours; dated the ——— day of ———.

The Declaration of Independence

Articles of Capitulation agreed on between Capt. Charles Hudson of His Brittannic Majestys Navy & Lieut. Colonel Scott Commandant of Fort Moultrie on the surrender of that Fort May 7th 1780 —

1 — That the Troops in Garrison be allowed to march out with the usual honours of War —

Granted & to pile their arms outside of the Gate

2 — That all the officers in Garrison as well Continental as Militia & the non commissioned officers & privates of the Militia shall be consi=dered as prisoners of War at large on parole untill exchanged and be allowed in the mean time to reside with their Families & Friends —

Every humanity shall be shewn to sick & well

The Fort, Artillery, Arms, Ammunition & Stores of all kinds to be delivered up to such Officers & Guards as Capt Hudson shall think proper to send for the purpose

The Garrison to march out of the Fort & pile their arms early this morning in front of the Brittish Forces who will be drawn up before the entrance of the Fort on the occasion

Charles Hudson
Wm Scott Lt Colo 1 Regmt
& Commandant of
Fort Moultrie

Part of the Articles of Capitulation agreed on at the surrender of Fort Moultrie

By the KING.

A PROCLAMATION,

Declaring the Ceffation of Arms, as well by Sea as Land, agreed upon between His Majefty, the Moft Chriftian King, the King of *Spain*, the States General of the *United Provinces*, and the United States of *America*, and enjoining the Obfervance thereof.

GEORGE R.

WHEREAS Provifional Articles were figned at *Paris*, on the Thirtieth Day of *November* laft, between Our Commiffioner for treating of Peace with the Commiffioners of the United States of *America*, and the Commiffioners of the faid States, to be inferted in and to conftitute the Treaty of Peace propofed to be concluded between Us, and the faid United States, when Terms of Peace fhould be agreed upon between Us and His Moft Chriftian Majefty: And whereas Preliminaries for reftoring Peace between Us and His Moft Chriftian Majefty, were figned at *Verfailles* on the Twentieth Day of *January* laft, by the Minifters of Us and the Moft Chriftian King. And whereas Preliminaries for reftoring Peace between Us and the King of *Spain*, were alfo figned at *Verfailles*, on the Twentieth Day of *January* laft, between the Minifters of Us and the King of *Spain*: And whereas, for putting an End to the Calamity of War as foon and as far as may be poffible, it hath been agreed between Us, His Moft Chriftian Majefty, the King of *Spain*, the States-General of the *United Provinces*, and the United States of *America*, as follows, that is to fay,

THAT fuch Veffels and Effects as fhould be taken in the *Channel* and in the *North Seas*, after the Space of Twelve Days, to be computed from the Ratification of the faid Preliminary Articles, fhould be reftored on all Sides; That the Term fhould be One Month from the *Channel* and the *North Seas* as far as the *Canary Iflands* inclufively, whether in the Ocean or in the *Mediterranean*; Two Months from the faid *Canary Iflands* as far as the Equinoctial Line or Equator; and laftly, Five Months in all other Parts of the World, without any Exception, or any other more particular Defcription of Time or Place.

AND whereas the Ratifications of the faid Preliminary Articles between Us and the Moft Chriftian King, in due Form, were exchanged by the Minifters of Us and of the Moft Chriftian King, on the Third Day of this inftant *February*; and the Ratifications of the faid Preliminary Articles between Us and the King of *Spain*, were exchanged between the Minifters of Us and of the King of *Spain*, on the Ninth Day of this inftant *February*; from which Days refpectively the feveral Terms above-mentioned, of Twelve Days, of One Month, of Two Months, and of Five Months, are to be computed: And whereas it is Our Royal Will and Pleafure that the Ceffation of Hoftilities between Us and the States General of the *United Provinces*, and the United States of *America*, fhould be agreeable to the Epochs fixed between Us and the Moft Chriftian King:

WE have thought fit, by and with the Advice of Our Privy Council, to notify the fame to all Our loving Subjects, and We do declare, that Our Royal Will and Pleafure is, and we do hereby ftrictly charge and command all Our Officers, both at Sea and Land, and all other Our Subjects whatfoever, to forbear all Acts of Hoftility, either by Sea or Land, againft His Moft Chriftian Majefty, the King of *Spain*, the States General of the *United Provinces*, and the United States of *America*, their Vaffals or Subjects, from and after the refpective Times above-mentioned, and under the Penalty of incurring Our higheft Difpleafure.

Given at Our Court at St. James's, *the Fourteenth Day of* February, *in the Twenty-third Year of Our Reign, and in the Year of Our Lord One Thoufand, Seven Hundred and Eighty-three.*

GOD fave the KING.

The Treaty of Paris in 1783 ended the Revolutionary War.

151

Colonial America Time Line

Before the arrival of Europeans, many millions of Indians belonging to dozens of tribes lived in North America (and also in Central and South America)

About 982 A.D.—Eric the Red, born in Norway, reaches Greenland during one of the first European voyages to North America

About 985—Eric the Red brings settlers from Iceland to Greenland

About 1000—Leif Ericson (Eric the Red's son) leads what is thought to be the first European expedition to mainland North America; Leif probably lands in Canada

1492—Christopher Columbus, sailing for Spain, reaches America

1497—John Cabot reaches Canada in the first English voyage to North America

1513—Ponce de León of Spain explores Florida

1519-1521—Hernando Cortés of Spain conquers Mexico

1565—St. Augustine, Florida, the first permanent European town in what is now the United States, is founded by the Spanish

1607—Jamestown, Virginia is founded, the first permanent English town in the present-day U.S.

1608—Frenchman Samuel de Champlain founds the village of Quebec, Canada

1609—Henry Hudson explores the eastern coast of present-day U.S. for The Netherlands; the Dutch then claim parts of New York, New Jersey, Delaware, and Connecticut and name the area New Netherland

1619—Virginia's House of Burgesses, America's first representative lawmaking body, is founded

1619—The first shipment of black slaves arrives in Jamestown

1620—English Pilgrims found Massachusetts' first permanent town at Plymouth

1621—Massachusetts Pilgrims and Indians hold the famous first Thanksgiving feast in colonial America

1622—Indians kill 347 settlers in Virginia

1623—Colonization of New Hampshire is begun by the English

1624—Colonization of present-day New York State is begun by the Dutch at Fort Orange (Albany)

1625—The Dutch start building New Amsterdam (now New York City)

1630—The town of Boston, Massachusetts is founded by the English Puritans

1633—Colonization of Connecticut is begun by the English

1634—Colonization of Maryland is begun by the English

1635—Boston Latin School, the colonies' first public school, is founded

1636—Harvard, the colonies' first college, is founded in Massachusetts

1636—Rhode Island colonization begins when Englishman Roger Williams founds Providence

1638—The colonies' first library is established at Harvard

1638—Delaware colonization begins when Swedish people build Fort Christina at present-day Wilmington

1640—Stephen Daye of Cambridge, Massachusetts prints *The Bay Psalm Book*, the first English-language book published in what is now the U.S.

1643—Swedish settlers begin colonizing Pennsylvania

1647—Massachusetts forms the first public school system in the colonies

1650—North Carolina is colonized by Virginia settlers in about this year

1650—Population of colonial U.S. is about 50,000

1660—New Jersey colonization is begun by the Dutch at present-day Jersey City

1670—South Carolina colonization is begun by the English near Charleston

1673—Jacques Marquette and Louis Jolliet explore the upper Mississippi River for France

1675-76—New England colonists beat Indians in King Philip's War

1682—Philadelphia, Pennsylvania is settled

1682—La Salle explores Mississippi River all the way to its mouth in Louisiana and claims the whole Mississippi Valley for France

1693—College of William and Mary is founded in Williamsburg, Virginia

1700—Colonial population is about 250,000

1704—*The Boston News-Letter*, the first successful newspaper in the colonies, is founded

1706—Benjamin Franklin is born in Boston

1732—George Washington, future first president of the United States, is born in Virginia

1733—English begin colonizing Georgia, their thirteenth colony in what is now the United States

1735—John Adams, future second president, is born in Massachusetts

1743—Thomas Jefferson, future third president, is born in Virginia

1750—Colonial population is about 1,200,000

1754—France and England begin fighting the French and Indian War over North American lands

1763—England, victorious in the war, gains Canada and most other French lands east of the Mississippi River

1764—British pass Sugar Act to gain tax money from the colonists

1765—British pass the Stamp Act, which the colonists despise; colonists then hold the Stamp Act Congress in New York City

1766—British repeal the Stamp Act

1770—British soldiers kill five Americans in the "Boston Massacre"

1773—Colonists dump British tea into Boston Harbor at the "Boston Tea Party"

1774—British close up port of Boston to punish the city for the tea party

1774—Delegates from all the colonies but Georgia meet in Philadelphia at the First Continental Congress

1775—**April 19:** Revolutionary war begins at Lexington and Concord, Massachusetts

May 10: Second Continental Congress convenes in Philadelphia

June 17: Colonists inflict heavy losses on British but lose Battle of Bunker Hill near Boston

July 3: George Washington takes command of Continental army

1776—**March 17:** Washington's troops force the British out of Boston in the first major American win of the war

May 4: Rhode Island is first colony to declare itself independent of Britain

July 4: Declaration of Independence is adopted

December 26: Washington's forces win Battle of Trenton (New Jersey)

1777—January 3: Americans win at Princeton, New Jersey

August 16: Americans win Battle of Bennington at New York-Vermont border

September 11: British win Battle of Brandywine Creek near Philadelphia

September 26: British capture Philadelphia

October 4: British win Battle of Germantown near Philadelphia

October 17: About 5,000 British troops surrender at Battle of Saratoga in New York

December 19: American army goes into winter quarters at Valley Forge, Pennsylvania, where more than 3,000 of them die by spring

1778—February 6: France joins the American side

July 4: American George Rogers Clark captures Kaskaskia, Illinois from the British

1779—February 23-25: George Rogers Clark captures Vincennes in Indiana

September 23: American John Paul Jones captures British ship *Serapis*

1780—May 12: British take Charleston, South Carolina

August 16: British badly defeat Americans at Camden, South Carolina

October 7: Americans defeat British at Kings Mountain, South Carolina

1781—January 17: Americans win battle at Cowpens, South Carolina

March 1: Articles of Confederation go into effect as laws of the United States

March 15: British suffer heavy losses at Battle of Guilford Courthouse in North Carolina; British then give up most of North Carolina

October 19: British army under Charles Cornwallis surrenders at Yorktown, Virginia as major revolutionary war fighting ends

1783—September 3: United States officially wins Revolution as the United States and Great Britain sign Treaty of Paris

November 25: Last British troops leave New York City

1787—On December 7, Delaware becomes the first state by approving the U.S. Constitution

1788—On June 21, New Hampshire becomes the ninth state when it approves the U.S. Constitution; with nine states having approved it, the Constitution goes into effect as the law of the United States

1789—On April 30, George Washington is inaugurated as first president of the United States

1790—On May 29, Rhode Island becomes the last of the original thirteen colonies to become a state

1791—U.S. Bill of Rights goes into effect on December 15

About the Author

Dennis Brindell Fradin is the author of more than 100 published children's books. His works for Childrens Press include the Young People's Stories of Our States series, the Disaster! series, and the Thirteen Colonies series. His other books are *Remarkable Children* (Little, Brown), which is about twenty children who made history, and a science-fiction novel entitled *How I Saved the World* (Dillon). Dennis is married to Judith Bloom Fradin, a high-school English teacher. They have two sons named Tony and Mike and a daughter named Diana Judith. Dennis was graduated from Northwestern University in 1967 with a B.A. in creative writing, and has lived in Evanston, Illinois, since that year.

Photo Credits